FROM THE PRAIRIE
TO THE
MOUNTAINS

FROM THE PRAIRIE
TO THE
MOUNTAINS

Altha Earnest

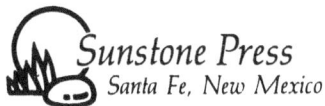

Sunstone Press
Santa Fe, New Mexico

DEDICATION

"Now also when I am old and grey-headed, O God, forsake me not, until I have showed thy strength, and thy power to everyone that is to come." Psalm 71:18

This book is dedicated to "everyone that is to come:" my children, my grandchildren, and great-grandchildren. May they find peace.

ACKNOWLEDGMENTS

I am grateful to Phoebe Hummel for typing and editing this book, and to Janiece Ritter Cramer for all her help in getting the manuscript into book form.

First Edition

Printed in the United States of America

Library of Congress Cataloging in Publication Data:

Earnest, Altha, 1909-
    From the prairie to the mountains.

    Includes index.
    1. Earnest, Altha, 1909-   . 2. New Mexico--
Biography. 3. Oklahoma--Biography. I. Title.
CT275.E225A3   1987   976.6'04'0924 (B)   87-1907
ISBN: 0-86534-107-9

Published in 1987 by SUNSTONE PRESS
                Post Office Box 2321
                Santa Fe, NM 87504-2321 / USA

CONTENTS

Chapter 1
ALL THE RELATIVES

Remembering My Grandparents
THE WRIGHTS

Before it became a state, Oklahoma was divided into territories. The larger portion was called Indian Territory and west of that was Oklahoma Territory. Indian Territory was supposed to be for the Indians when they were forced out of their homes east of the Mississippi. The Trail of Tears ended there. However, whites began settling in the Indian Territory, or anywhere else they could find land.

The Oklahoma Run in April 1889 opened up even more unclaimed (by whites) land for settlement. People lined up at the border on horseback and in buggies and wagons. At the signal they ran forward and found the parcels they liked, quickly staking out the boundaries. In 1907 Oklahoma became a state.

My father's father, John Perry Wright, did not take part in the Run. He moved to Oklahoma from Caldwell County, Missouri, in 1898 and bought a farm already established. He was about 60 years old and must have been financially prosperous because he had enough money to buy a more fertile and desirable creek bottom farm.

John Perry Wright was born in 1838 in McCracken County, Kentucky. He married Elizabeth Woodbury, from Athens County, Ohio, in 1861. She was two years older than her husband and the story goes that she taught him to read. They may have had an adventuresome life, living in Nebraska and Missouri. There is a story about

Elizabeth's father going to California and on to Australia during the Gold Rush. I leave it to any of the family who cares to go back into the history of these grandparents. I'll stay with Oklahoma!

Within ten years my grandfather had made his creek bottom farm into a prosperous homestead and had hired hands to help him with the heavy work. He built a big white two-story house with green trim to replace the original farmhouse on the property. In those days people bought materials for these homes, gingerbread and all, from mail-order catalogues.

The house had a wrap-around porch, a parlor with a large leaded glass window and an upstairs balcony in back. In the parlor there was a pump organ and a Victrola with a "He knows his master's voice" horn that looked like a big morning glory. There were records all the way from "Uncle Josh Puts up the Stove Pipe" to the Great Caruso.

My grandmother loved flowers and surrounded the house with them. I especially remember the morning glories.

Separate from the house was the milk house. It was kept cool by water which was pumped into a trough which ran through the building and continued on down the hill. Milk and cream were chilled there, as well as fruit.

A windmill pumped water for the household and livestock. There were horse barns, long troughs for the animals to drink from, a blacksmith shop and implement house. A big iron bell at the back of the main house called the farm folk to dinner. My grandfather had the only wagon-sized scales in the county. People would come by with a wagonload of farm produce, drive onto the scales, get weighed and then go to market.

There were several acres of locust trees. These were for shade, for fence posts and when they bloomed in the summer, the smell was heavenly! There were grapevine swings near the swimming hole.

My grandfather had the latest in farm equipment. The large cow barn had the best stanchions for holding the cows while they were milked. When cousins came to visit we played in the hay barns and jumped from one level to the next, enjoying the sweet smell of alfalfa.

To top it all off, there was a row of tiny chicken nests built to match the main house — white with green trim and shingled roofs. Inside, each hen had a china egg for a nest egg to encourage her to lay more. The chickens were called Dormernickers.

One cousin called all this an estate. I called it a kingdom.

My Grandfather and Grandmother Wright had ten children, six sons and four daughters. Of the sons, Sam and Dan were twins; of the daughters, Belle and Delle were twins. Three of the daughters married Hall brothers. In 1892, at about 25 years of age, Aunt Ellen married Ulysses Grant Hall and Aunt Mary, about 21, married William Hall in a double wedding at the brides' home in Catawba, Missouri. In 1902, Aunt Delle married Zeph Hall in Washita County, Oklahoma.

Uncle Zeph was a prosperous farmer, very generous with his family. My first ride in an automobile was with him. He had a 1914 Ford touring car with mica windows in the side curtains to use during rain or snow.

After Aunt Delle died, some sixty years later, Uncle Zeph was getting feeble, and he decided to live with daughter Myrtle and her husband, Leland Smith. He had not kept up with how things were changing and said to Myrtle, "Now I want to pay my way if I stay here. I'm going to pay you one dollar a day." Myrtle, who was well-to-do, took what he offered, knowing he could not understand how the world had changed.

When I was nine years old my Grandmother Wright died. It was a Sunday morning, and we were all dressed to go to church at Port. The phone rang, and it was Grandfather telling us to come. When we arrived, Grandmother was dead of a heart attack. She was eighty-three. Her body lay in state in the parlor. Later the hearse was drawn by horses to the funeral service at Port Methodist Church and burial in the Port cemetery.

After her death Grandfather Wright thought of retirement. He rented the farm and he and Belle moved to Carter, a small town nearby. That move didn't work out for some reason, and they moved to Sentinel.

Grandfather had been in the army during the Civil War. All his life he drew a small disability pension. I asked my mother about that, and she said he had had measles while in the service and this damaged

9

his kidneys. He fought on the Northern side and usually voted Republican during his lifetime.

In Sentinel he and some of the older men would sit on benches downtown and discuss politics. The Ku Klux Klan was just coming in through the country and some had visited our community. In full robes they marched into our churches and frightened the citizens. They stopped and questioned a young couple riding home after church in a buggy.

When the elders of the town defended this by saying, "They are full-blooded Americans," Grandfather answered forcefully, "No full-blooded Americans are ashamed to show their faces."

He sometimes expounded, "If Congress appropriates money for this, or that, or that, we are headed for trouble."

I had never heard words like "appropriate" and "Congress." Since he no longer had the responsibility of the farm, he took his politics quite seriously. He was usually very reasonable, but as he grew older he developed some unusual prejudices.

He didn't like girls' hair cut with bangs over the forehead. Once Myrtle Hall came to Sentinal to have her high school graduation photo made. She stopped by to see her grandfather. Aunt Belle quickly took her out back to see the garden, lest Grandfather express his thoughts on bangs. Once Aunt Belle said she was going shopping and was it all right if she got a new spring hat? "Certainly," said Grandfather, "but buy a *hat*, not one of those bird's nest looking things."

As my grandfather grew older, he spent most of his days in bed. Dr. Bennett lived two blocks down the street, and every morning he would make a call on Grandfather. This must have gone on for a year or more. I don't know whether they discussed health or politics.

Grandfather died at the age of eighty-nine at home in Sentinel. Funeral services were at the Methodist Church. An American flag was draped on the casket. Rev. Ellis read the 103rd Psalm. As the funeral procession passed downtown Sentinel, all stores were closed in respect. He was buried at Port Cemetery beside his wife Elizabeth and son Ira.

Rev. Ellis was from Retrop. He was pastor of a small church there, and in 1914 performed the marriage ceremony for my Aunt

Ethel and Uncle Dan Evans. Often the towns and churches die away, but the cemeteries are well kept and that is where many "go home" today.

Dr. Leonard Gillingham, now one of the shining lights in the Methodist hierarchy of the New Mexico Annual Conference, was a pastor at Retrop. Dr. Gillingham also conducted the funeral service for my Aunt Ellen Hall when she died at Sentinel in her ninety-first year.

And Then There Was
AUNT BELLE

Aunt Belle was a special person in my life. She spoiled me when I was a baby and encouraged me when I was growing up. She lent me books and magazines when there was nothing to read at home. When I was quite small, she would go shopping with my mother and me and the clerks would ask if Aunt Belle were my mother. In my seventies I still look like her.

She was Aunt Belle to a large clan. She lived with her parents and took care of her mother until she died, then she took care of her father until he died. Then she had the care of our Aunt Ellen until she died. She didn't marry until after her father died, when she was about fifty. In 1929 she married Jacob Wattenberger and was step-mother to his five children. Mr. Wattenberger died three years later but the stepchildren remained loyal to her as long as she lived.

She kept up with the birthdays of all her nieces and nephews, knew who they married and where they lived. When I was about ten, the Chautauqua came to Sentinel. She had me come stay with her, and we went to every program for one week. It was under a big tent. There must have been some lectures that were above my head for I remember very little. But the thing I do remember is that one was a play, "Peg O' My Heart." The leading lady came in carrying a shaggy dog in her arms and we all applauded like wild.

Cousin Foley Wright wrote her when he lived in Paris that he was singing in the choir at the American Church there. Aunt Belle took this item down to the *Sentinel Leader Weekly* and they printed it. And they printed other items she brought in from time to time. Some of my early efforts at writing poetry were printed. One of her favorite proverbs was, "He that tooteth not his own horn, his horn is not tooted."

Nephew Ona's son, Cecil, was born with a harelip and when the corrective surgery was done, Aunt Belle said, "I'll pay for it." Cecil was high school age when he drowned in a pond near Vaughn, New Mexico. Aunt Belle volunteered to pay for the funeral.

Aunt Belle died at eighty-four. She was in a nursing home in Elk City, where her nieces, Myrtle and Naomi, lived. They came to see her every day. The last letter she wrote to us from the nursing home was full of family news as usual. She was interested in everything. She wrote, "I don't think I need to be here, but that is the doctor's orders and I will abide by them." Some five weeks later she died. Her funeral service was at the Methodist Church in Sentinel.

My Other Grandparents
THE ADDINGTONS

My mother's mother, Altha Elizabeth Addington, was born in Boone County, Arkansas, May 18, 1854. Her mother was Martha Lucinda Smith. Martha Lucinda lived to be seventy-seven years old and is buried in Bentonville, Arkansas. My mother's grandfather was William Riley Addington, who died in 1863, at forty-one years of age. We don't know his final resting place.

I have the last letter my grandmother, Altha, wrote on August 27, 1897, at Fort Sill, Oklahoma. It begins, "My Dear Blessed Mama." As a postscript she wrote, "I have not got any wasted pieces at present." I take this to mean that my great grandmother was a quilter and needed more scraps of fabric, or "wasted pieces."

The children of William and Martha Addington were Cynthia Ann, Winifred Addeline, Texana Mathilde, China Jane, Altha Elizabeth, Mary Frances, and Robert Noel. I knew four of these great aunts, but not Aunt Tex. Cynthia Ann became Aunt Tent; Winifred Addeline, Aunt Ad; Texana, Aunt Tex; China Jane, Aunt China; and Mary Frances, Aunt Molly. Altha Elizabeth was to become my grandmother, but because she died so young, Aunt Ad became my real grandmother. We don't know what became of Robert Noel.

My grandmother, Altha, had been married four times and had

had eight children when she died at forty-three at Fort Sill, Oklahoma, in 1897. At eighteen she married C.A. Pierce, a retired captain of the Confederate Army. Their only child Annie was born in 1871. Annie Pierce married when she was about eighteen and had five children. She died when she was twenty-nine. She left Louella, Jesse, Clem, Tom Stewart, and Grace.

Grace is Grace Eno now, and is eighty-six years old. She married three times. To her first marriage was born her only child, Wanda. Grace now lives near her granddaughter, Carolyn, and her family in Oklahoma City.

Altha's second marriage was to a man named White, and they had one son, Robert A., born in 1877.

Her next marriage was to Henry P. McCune in 1880. Their children were twins Birdie and Lonnie, Ed, Goldie, Maudie, and Ethel. Lonnie died at age two months. Goldie was to become my mother.

Of my grandfather, Henry Perry McCune, we know little. We know that he came from Ohio and was born in 1854. We have a photo of his mother. It is a marvelous portrait by the Dayton Photo and View Co., Dayton, Ohio. Since they had roving photographers in those days that isn't much help in determining where she lived. She is standing in a very dignified pose, wearing a dress that looks as if made of silk, with a lace jabot. The photographer's studio probably supplied the lace curtains and cut velvet chair beside her.

In 1892 Henry McCune died suddenly of sunstroke while helping to build Fort Sill. Birdie, the oldest of his children, was eleven. At the burial service a friend wanted to play taps for Henry, even though he was a civilian. But the man couldn't finish. He broke down and wept, "Farewell, old comrade."

At Fort Sill my mother often saw Geronimo riding around in a surrey. Geronimo was a prisoner for many years at Fort Sill. There he was allowed to live much as he pleased. Later he married and had a family.

Altha's last marriage was to Jim J. Stewart. They had one son, Glen. Mr. Stewart was a cattle inspector around Fort Sill. Their cattle were branded with ALTH and in those days could roam free, identified only by brand.

13

Once I asked my mother, "Why did she marry so many times. Why did she marry Mr. Stewart?"

My mother answered, "In those days if you were left a widow with seven children, you married."

Mr. Stewart was left with one son and six stepchildren. Robert White was 21 and took responsibility for his four younger half sisters and brother. He took the five McCune children and traveled a long distance to Wahsita County to homestead a quarter section of land near the town of Port. He must have been a wonderful young man. Perhaps he had some help from the Jim Walker family who traveled with them in a covered wagon and who homesteaded nearby.

They did what most others were doing at the time. Homesteading meant building a home half-dug into the side of a hill and trying to make a living off the land. The McCunes and Walkers lived in the Port School dugout while their homes were being made. Later the children walked about two miles to this school.

Homesteading and caring for five children soon became too hard for Robert, and it was decided to send the three younger girls to the Buckner's Orphans Home in Dallas, Texas. This was a Baptist institution and is in operation today. The story goes that some of the Orphans Home staff met Robert and the girls part way so he wouldn't have to travel all the distance to Dallas. On his way back to the farm, Robert stopped to work at Marietta, Indian Territory, where he became ill and died at age twenty-two.

Birdie had stayed behind with the Walker family. At nineteen she married Henry Goines and went to live on the farm he homesteaded. Later they acquired Robert White's farm.

Ed didn't want to go to the orphan's home so he also stayed behind. Later he returned to Fort Sill where he lived most of his life. He is buried in Fort Sill along with his father, Henry, and mother, Altha. Altha's marker says "A.E. Stewart."

In 1925 the Addingtons decided to have a family reunion in Lookeba, Oklahoma, some thirty-eight miles east of Cordell. Aunt Tent came; she would have been about seventy-nine years old then. Some of her children and grandchildren came. Aunt Ad came from Nacona, Texas. She would have been seventy-seven, and she looked wonderful. Aunt China came; she was about sixty-five. Aunt Molly and her husband, Dow Covey, were there. She was sixty-three.

For three days, aunts, great aunts, cousins, second cousins and third cousins visited, ate, sang, and enjoyed themselves. We slept outdoors on the lawn since it was summertime.

They all loved music so the reunion had a theme song, "In the Morning of Joy." Aunt Molly brought her fiddle. She said if you played by note it was a violin and if you played by ear it was a fiddle. Aunt China brought her accordion. These two had played on some of the radio programs in Little Rock, Arkansas. The Addington sisters used to make up songs to popular tunes and sing them to one another.

Uncle Dow was a vice president of the American Trust Company of Little Rock. He had also been a state representative. Aunt Molly wasn't a shrinking violet. She told us that her grey crepe georgette beaded dress cost seventy-five dollars. Our eyes grew big. She rounded us up in the parlor, got out her Mary Baker Eddy book and began to read to us. We Baptist and Campbellites had never heard such. She would say, "Now isn't that just as simple and clear as can be?" We didn't find it simple nor clear, but we listened with respect because it was Aunt Molly.

We all had a wonderful time at that family reunion.

Letter written by my grandmother McCune in 1897. She died three weeks after writing this.

Fort Sill Okla   Aug 27 1897

My dear blessed mama

Your card to hand, glad indeed to hear you were all well, this leaves us all in good health.

Well, Ma we made a short visit up to Annie's. We were gone 2 weeks and 1 day. It was such a long, rough trip in the hot but we seen lots of country and it was nice for the children and it was so much pleasure to be with Annie. We only stayed with her 2 days and 2 nights.

Ad was sick and 1 of the children was not well. I would not live there if they would give me the country. It is big timber and awful rich country. They have raised a fine crop and may not be able to gather it. They are in bad shape, but if they would be well they could make it all right.

They have plenty to eat and lots of hay and a very good team.

Mr. Stewart give them 10 dollars.

Bob and Ed left the house for while and was gone. We are talking of moving next year about 40 miles from here to the Chickasaw on account of schooling. I would rather (live) in this country as anywhere, but there is no showing for any school at all. Our cotton is doing fine. The children got to see apples on the trees. We bought some . . . seeds. First I had seen since '75. I am afraid Will and Lou made a bad move. Do you know where Carl and Tent aims to winter?

Tell Tex I will be glad to get a letter from her. I hope her health is much better. Mollie sent me the pictures . . . thought she looked much better than she did in the last one she sent me. Ma I would be glad to have a late picture of yours and I want to have it enlarged. So write soon and all the news.

Your daug
Alth Stewart

I have not got any wasted pieces at present.

MY MOTHER AND FATHER

My mother, Goldie, must have been about twelve when she entered Buckner's Orphan Home. Maudie was about ten and Ethel was about seven. Little Maudie died two years later but Goldie and Ethel were raised there.

When a girl was eighteen she could leave if there were a relative to go to. My mother went to live with her sister Birdie and her husband Henry Goines. Ethel followed when she was about sixteen. My mother said she could hardly wait until she was reunited with her baby sister. Later on, when my mother married, Ethel went to live with her.

At the orphanage my mother and aunt received good Christian training. My mother learned hundreds of songs and hymns by memory. She sang all the songs she learned there and also cowboy songs, "After the Ball," "The Bonnie Wee Widow," "Won't You Come Home Bill Bailey?" and others. In those days people made up words to popular tunes. One song my mother taught me was "Red Wings." Thirty-five years later my sons were taking piano lessons and playing "The Happy Farmer" to the tune of "Red Wings."

To me and all my brothers and my sister my mother sang this lullaby, written by Isaac Watts, 1674-1748. He wrote several hundred hymns, including "Joy to the World," "God, Our Help in Ages Past." I sang this to all my children and grandchildren. It is sung to the tune of "Come Thou Fount."

A Cradle Hymn

Hush my babe, lie still in slumber
Holy angels guard thy bed!
Heavenly blessings without number
Gently falling on thy head.

How much better thou art 'tended
Than the Son of God could be
When from heaven he descended
and became a child like thee.

Soft and easy in thy cradle
Coarse and hard thy Saviour lay
For his birth place was a manger
And his softest bed was hay.

Oh, to tell the wondrous stories
How the foes abused our King,
How they killed the Lord of Glory
Makes me angry while I sing.

Hush, my babe, I did not chide thee
Tho' my song may seem so hard
Tis thy mother sits beside thee
And her arms shall be thy guard.

Mayst thou live to love and know Him,
Trust and serve Him all thy days,
Then to dwell forever near him,
Tell his love and sing his praise.

At our farm my mother sang to the cows and horses. She spent hours petting and talking to them. She knew all their birthdays. In fact, she remembered the animals' birthdays more than those of her children. "Belle can keep up with those," she said.

My mother always wore a dress and sunbonnet when she work-ed in the fields. The cows wouldn't let anybody else milk them. One

17

time when we went to visit Uncle Jim McCune the boys stayed home to do the milking. They had to wear her dresses and bonnets so that the cows would let them milk!

She loved being outside and doing hard work more than anything. In fact, when she was seventy, she pulled cotton for some spending money.

Men who traded in cows and horses would come to the farm and she liked to bargain with them. She would talk to the traders for hours. My father wouldn't have anything to do with them. My father never touched a cow — never!

In some ways she was ahead of her time. When relatives and friends would tell about what caused a certain birthmark, saying the mother was frightened by this or that, my mother would look at them in silence. Before I was born my mother went to the funeral of a dear neighbor. People told her that she shouldn't look at Mrs. Map in death, as that might harm the unborn. My mother said she didn't believe in superstitions.

My father, Charles Peter Wright, was born February 19, 1869. He grew up on a farm, so he became a farmer. That's what most people did then.

Charles married Minnie Rayner and they had two sons, Cecil David and Ona Boyd. When the two boys were small, Cecil and their mother died of a fever. The young widower turned to his parents for help in raising Ona, and thus Ona grew up in the kingdom. Aunt Belle doted on him and Grandmother Wright thought he could do no wrong. When Charles decided to marry again, Ona stayed with his grandparents and Aunt Belle. Ona was married at nineteen to Julia Atchison.

In 1908 Charles Wright met Goldie Agnes McCune and they married February 28, 1909. Because of his father's prosperity and standing in the community, Charles was considered quite a catch. In those days if you got to be twenty-three years old and weren't married, you were getting to be an old maid. My mother thought all her life that being an old maid was one of the biggest disgraces in this whole wide world. She was twenty-three years old when she got married; my father was forty. Some ten months later I came along.

Chapter 2
GROWING UP ON THE FARM IN OKLAHOMA

I was spoiled by everyone, Aunt Ethel, Aunt Belle, and other aunts and uncles. My first baby picture was taken with Aunt Ethel holding me. My very earliest memory is of Aunt Ethel giving a party in our front room. There were boxes placed along the walls, boards were laid over these and then padded by folded quilts. I was about three years old. When I toddled into the room, everyone wanted me to come to them! I don't remember how I got out of that room, but I do remember the incident plainly, the first time I made an entrance.

I've always talked a lot, probably because I was born tongue tied. At birth, my tongue was attached to the bottom of my mouth with a tiny membrane that had to be clipped, otherwise it might have caused a speech impediment. My father always said the doctor cut it too much and made my tongue loose at both ends!

This must have been inherited because Aunt Belle talked with a slight lisp. Later on our son Stephen had this, and his son Jeffrey. None of them had any trouble talking either!

One day my mother was in the kitchen singing, "I'm in the Gloryland Way." My father had called Aunt Belle on the telephone and was holding me up to talk to her. He said, "Say something to your Aunt Belle."

I said, "We've got gloryland over at our house."

Every Sunday we dressed up in our "Sunday-go-to-meetin'" clothes and went to the Baptist church in Port. We rode in the buggy and I can still remember the smell of our freshly starched dresses and the men's starched shirts. Mrs. Baker, wife of our country doctor, was my Sunday school teacher. We met behind the piano with a curtain on one side. Our lessons were taught from colored cards printed with Bible pictures and verses. A poster-sized picture was given as a prize to the pupil having the best lesson. After I had taken two or three of these home, Mrs. Baker said, "Let someone besides Altha take home the big picture today." I don't know if I was the most brilliant, but I talked a lot!

In 1918 my grandfather bought a car. It may have been a Maxwell. It was a large touring car and had belonged to Dr. Shadid in Carter. The doctor's initials were on the sides, and somehow one of his old bags had been left in the car. Our family used that bag for years.

Dr. Shadid later moved to Elk City where he established a community hospital in the nineteen-thirties. Each family paid so much each year and then their medical expenses were taken care of. I remember the other doctors fighting this in the newspapers or in any way they could. After this Dr. Shadid was written up in the *Reader's Digest*. He was ahead of his time.

Sometimes friends and neighbors gathered around a quilting frame and "got out" a quilt. Little girls would slip under the quilt and listen to the women talk. My friend says that is where she learned the facts of life. One mother with four small children said, "If John only hangs his pants at the foot of the bed, I get pregnant." Some of the information we garnered was puzzling!

One of the topics the ladies enjoyed was how to cut up a chicken. Since chicken was a staple, they spent time on that subject. I found it boring and somehow managed to avoid learning to butcher a chicken.

As youngsters we often went to our parents with a little bruise, a tiny cut or a scraped knee. Our parents would examine the injury seriously and say, "It will feel better when it quits hurting." I would like to say that some of these children who received that diagnosis grew up to be doctors and used that same soothing tone on their small patients.

I was born on the farm my father owned one-half mile north and adjoining Grandfather Wright's farm. My father struggled to make a living on that farm. Crab grass grew better than the cotton crop. My mother called it "that old sand hill." Cows and chickens were our main source of income. I remember when we bought a cream separator. After that we went to town once a week with large cans of cream to sell.

We had a field of alfalfa and one of corn. I often watched our herd of cows grazing on the stubby pasture and gazing hungrily at the beautiful, luscious fields of corn and alfalfa. One day the cows got organized. They gathered at the fence and pushed at the same time. Down went the fence! By the time my father and mother came to the rescue, some of the cows were bloated with the green food. I'll always remember my mother with a butcher knife stabbing a big bloated cow in the side, trying to save its life. Most of the time a bloated cow meant the loss of that cow.

We had pork in winter and chicken in the summer to eat. We often had biscuits three times a day. Occasionally there was a pan of cornbread. A German neighbor baked bread made with yeast. My people called it "light bread" and my uncle said "it is the best smell I ever smelt."

After Grandmother Wright died and Grandfather retired to Sentinel, he decided that his farm would be rented to Charlie. So my father sold his farm and we moved into the big house that had been my second home all my life.

I loved the big house, but more than that, I loved Sentinel. It was *town*. (The population was less than a thousand.) You walked to church, you went downtown for the mail. If you walked at night, you could see into people's living rooms. Aunt Belle and Grand-father had a bookcase full of books, and they subscribed to some wonderful magazines, all of which I wanted to read.

My parents started going to a Church of Christ in Sentinel which did not believe in Sunday School, and had other unusual prac-tices. At that time the Church of Christ would have debates. The whole family, seven of us, once spent a whole week attending a debate at Rocky. We would work in the fields all day, then drive some seventeen miles to hear two ministers argue whether we should serve communion using one cup or two cups. The debate would sometimes get nasty. One minister would ridicule the other for saying, "and he 'tuck' the cup," instead of saying "took." In later years my mother would go to a congregation that held one set of beliefs and my father to another.

No matter what their church affiliation, people would get together for singing conventions — Baptists, Methodists, Mennonites from Corn, Oklahoma, and those who had no church home. The conventions were held every month at school houses. There were notices in the weekly papers. For weeks before a singing we planned what we would wear that day.

The song books were of gospel songs. I remember an Indian from Gotebo singing "Look Down, Look Down That Long Lonesome Road, Before You Travel On." It was not in a book that we used. His voice was good.

Every home had hopes of an upright piano. If you could find a teacher, your daughter took piano lessons, which were paid for with egg and cream money. You had reached the height of your ambition if, at the singing convention, a song leader would choose you to play the piano. "Mary Agnes, will you come play for us?" Not at the Academy Awards would there be any more excitement, joy and honor than when Mary Agnes marched up to the piano.

The Church of Christ song books had "shaped notes." You had to attend a singing school in order to know how to sing from shaped notes. When Linda Belle, a darling young high school student, was asked to play for Mr. Misenhammer, page 52, in *Joyful Songs*, Linda Belle said, "I can't play those shaped notes."

In some communities the singing was more for fun than competition. There would be church on Sunday, dinner on the ground, and singing all afternoon. Other Sundays people would cook extra, put on pretty embroidered pillow cases to give the house a Sunday look, and after services you asked your friends and neighbors, "Come, go home with us."

Then it was back home and another week in the fields. Mr. Evans, our neighbor, always wore his Sunday white shirt on Monday as he plowed his fields. Probably wash day at the Evans' was on Tuesday. White clothes were boiled. Then they were rubbed on the scrub board, washed in lye soap, rinsed in blueing and starch and then hung outside on the line to dry. Clothes washed by that system smelled wonderful!

My mother had five children in eleven years. I was the first. Aunt Ethel named me — Altha Love.

Then came Cleo, whom we called "Clete." Cleo died of cancer in 1972 at Veterans Hospital in Albuquerque.

After him was Orville. Aunt Belle named him for one of the airplane inventors. Robert, Bob, was named for Robert La Follette. A few years later Robert La Follette ran for president. Grace was the last, born in the big hosue.

In those days babies were delivered at home, and the mother stayed in bed a full ten days. During that time someone had to come and care for the family. When my brother Orville was born, I wasn't yet five years old, so we needed help. A cousin, Altha Louella Hamon, came to care for us. We called her Ellie. She was happy and full of life. Her mother, Annie Pierce Hamon, had died at the age of twenty-nine, leaving Louella, the oldest, and four more little Hamons. So Louella knew about caring for little ones. Fortunately, there was always a relative to call upon at these times of need.

My father and mother couldn't run that big farm without help, and that required cash they didn't have. They tried, but after about two years, my father realized that he couldn't handle that rich, rich farm.

So he decided to move south to a little farm in Kiowa County. We called it "The Kiowa." Then we became renters. In the hierarchy of farming, if you were owner of a farm, especially a prosperous farm, you were at the top; then came the renters. At the bottom were the sharecroppers, which was just another word for slavery. My father never was a sharecropper.

For the next ten years my family lived in that three-room house in The Kiowa. We grew cotton, wheat, and maize, and we had cows, horses, pigs, chickens, and turkeys. I hated the whole thing!

I shocked wheat, I chopped cotton, I picked cotton. A horse-drawn mower cut the wheat and dropped bundles tied with binding twine on the ground. These had to be put in standing position in neat shocks and await the time when the threshing machine would decide to come to your house and thresh your crop.

With the threshing machine came the cook shack. We always enjoyed visiting the lady who cooked at the cook shack. The sides were let down to become tables to eat from. The men ate standing up. At the end of the day, my father and the men took wagon loads of wheat to town to be sold, often driving back after dark. Of course, if we had a good crop the prices were low, and if the hail or cyclones made for a small yield, prices were high. I never knew a time when this was not true.

Someone said cotton farming took thirteen months out of the year. Some forty-five years later, during the hippie years, I had a delightful friend helping me. She and her husband were living in a tiny Spanish-speaking community, trying to raise goats and chickens and live off the land. She began to question me when she knew I was raised on a farm. "When do chickens molt? For how long?" Finally she said, "Why did you leave all of that, Mrs. Earnest? Were you bored?"

I lived there for some six years until I entered high school at age twenty-two. Why did it take me so long? There were several reasons. One was that my parents weren't interested in education. My father said that back when they had McGuffey Readers you could get an education. Now, he said, it was a lot of basketball games and such nonsense.

We lived about eight miles from the nearest high school, and there were no school busses from our farm to the school. My father farmed with horses. He didn't have a car. I would have had to board with a family in some town with a high school, and my mother said they couldn't afford it. Besides, she said I would just get married anyway. I had no way out.

My mother wanted me to marry a farmer and settle down near her. I would have none of it. Some of my friends had married at sixteen, but after I passed that age, she gave up on the idea that I would marry the first fellow that came along. Once a neighbor asked, "What's the matter with Altha that she isn't married?"

"Well," my mother said, "she says that the Lord is going to dangle down her a husband from heaven." (And He did!)

In the meantime I read books. I would go to Hobart, the county seat, go to the library, get a few books, sit up at night and read by a kerosene lamp. Books could be returned by mail. I read Jean Stratton Porter's *The Keeper of the Bees* and others by her. I read Bess Streeter

Aldrich, Sinclair Lewis, Lloyd Douglas and Willa Cather. and I read my Bible, and sometimes memorized parts of it. I had to hang onto some kind of promise for a future.

My mother fussed at me all the time about the reading. The house would be a mess, and it would be my job to clean it. I'd go off into the bedroom and sit down and read. Of course, hundreds of girls have done that. I can still hear her saying, "Get to cleaning up this house and quit reading all the time."

I would go and spend a week with my Aunt Ethel or Aunt Birdie. I once spent a month or two at Lawton. I worked for a few weeks as a maid at Fort Sill. I also worked for a short time for a lady in the alteration department at a store. I knew how to sew because we made all our clothes at home on an old Singer treadle machine.

Once while staying with Aunt Birdie, she was asked to keep a minister, Lum Hall, who was coming to Retrop to hold a revival. A minister had to stay in someone's home during the ten days or two weeks of the revival. My cousin Faye and I had long talks with him. He was from Tennessee and had a wonderful sense of humor. He had a Southern accent; he thought life was wonderful. He saw that I knew my Bible, that life wasn't exactly kind to me, and somehow made me feel that there was hope, that I could be "somebody." When Faye and Sam Cluck were married a few years later, they went to Elk City to Lum Hall for the ceremony.

And I had the Bethel Church. Some three miles from our home was a Methodist church. The first time I saw it, all alone out on the prairie, I thought it was something beautiful. It looked good to me as I was starved for good literature, music, and activities. We had picnics, parties, ice cream socials, wiener roasts. Once I was chosen to attend an Institute at Guthrie, Oklahoma. It was a convention of young church people. There I heard Dr. Hargett of the Boston Avenue Methodist Church of Tulsa, and other interesting speakers. I have a photo taken one Sunday of the Bethel congregation, and there were 175 people present.

One large family that attended regularly was the Webb family. They had Bill, Lois (my age), Jessie, and on down the line, and finally to little Jacob. Someone was always carrying little Jacob around. Sometimes the family came in more than one car. Babies went to sleep at evening services. One night the family, looking for baby Jacob, decided as they got into the cars that no one had him. They went back into the church and there he was, fast asleep on a pallet.

We had programs for different holidays. At an Armistice Day program, my brother Bob donned a doughboy outfit and sang, "Good-bye Ma, Good-bye Pa, Good-bye Mule With the Old Hee Haw." We celebrated Christmas with a play, a tree and goodies. And Easter was not just another Sunday. We had plays that we sometimes presented at other churches. Orville and Helen Hall were living in that community, and the young people would sometimes meet in their home. Without Bethel, I don't see how I could have made it over those hard years.

Chapter 3
I FINALLY GO TO HIGH SCHOOL

Somewhere I saw the title to a book, *I Didn't Do It Alone.* Perhaps we can all say that. I know I have had some of the most unlikely, most unbelievable, benefactors in this world. For instance, there was one we shall call Mrs. Sherman. She was a character, a tyrant to her family and neighbors. And yet, she was the first person who opened the way for me to go to high school.

I never knew her first name. Few people did. She lived in a two-story brick house in a grove of trees, surrounded by lots of flowers. It was one of the nicer homes in that part of Western Oklahoma. Her furniture was lovely and her car was a new Buick. She considered herself a semi-invalid, but no one knew what was wrong with her.

Yes, there was a Mr. Sherman, Wirt Sherman. He was tall and lanky and he always seemed tired, as if he could hardly put one foot in front of the other. He was "all tuckered out," as they say in Oklahoma. Mrs. Sherman ruled the roost.

She was a member of the Church of Christ and felt that everyone else should be also. In the early days of the community, most people were either Baptist or Methodist. Both have lovely old white churches in the town of Port.

When I was eleven years old, a Brother Freeman came to Port and held a revival under a big tent. One Sunday Mrs. Sherman invited Brother Freeman and my parents, Charlie and Goldie, to her house for dinner. She and Brother Freeman explained the Church of Christ doctrine to my parents. The next night at the revival, the call went out to all who wanted to join the church. My father went to the front. Then my mother plumped Grace, my baby sister, into my lap and followed him. Grace began to cry, and I took her outside into the darkness and hushed her.

My parents were baptized in a creek. After that we met at Rock Front school house on Sundays for a short service. There was no pastor.

The story was told how Mrs. Sherman challenged one of the ministers at a revival. She stood up and said, "I'd like to know where *you* got *your* mourner's bench."

The evangelist pondered Mrs. Sherman's question. "Well, Sister, I believe we got it at the lumber yard."

In those days when you went up to the alter to repent of your sins, you knelt at the "mourner's bench" and said, perhaps not these words, but words with these meanings, "We acknowledge and bewail our manifold sins and wickedness, which we from time to time most grievously have committed by thought, word and deed, against Thy Divine Majesty. We do earnestly repent, and are heartily sorry for these, our misdoings; the remembrance of them is grievous unto us. Have mercy upon us, have mercy upon us, most merciful Father." Many a tear was shed at the "mourner's bench."

In a field near the Sherman's big house were some weatherbeaten house where two or three black families lived. They were probably sharecroppers. Mrs. Sherman got three or four of the women to meet with her in the parlor on Sunday mornings to partake of the Lord's Supper. It is not known what their previous church membership had been, but here they "knew their place," which was in Mrs. Sherman's parlor on Sunday mornings.

A young man in the group did not go along with this Sunday ritual. In fact, he seemed to have a mind of his own. Mrs. Sherman wouldn't let this pass. As a display of power, she bought a pistol, set up a target, and every evening did some target practice where young Zeke could see her. Still, he didn't appear at the Sunday service.

I knew these stories, and other stories, about Mrs. Sherman; but in spite of it all, one cold winter day while I was spending a week with my Aunt Birdie, we went to call on her. She began to question me and heard that I had never gone to high school. When she asked about this, I explained that we lived in a district where there were no school buses, and that my mother thought there wasn't any sense in going to school because I would just get married anyway.

I told her I had heard that girls could work their way through nursing school, so I wrote letters about this. I found out that the first thing you had to have was a high school diploma. Since finishing eighth grade, I had been working in the cotton fields. Depression time was upon us, and work of any kind was hard to find.

Mrs. Sherman then suggested that I come and stay with her and attend Port Consolidated High School.

I said, "I know about that. If you are over 21, you can't go to a public school in this state without paying tuition."

She replied, "They need not know how old you are."

I grabbed onto that straw. With all my heart I grabbed at that straw!

I knew Mrs. Sherman was tough. I knew that I was tough. During the seven years since I had finished grammar school and fought against a blank wall, I had memorized several poems, one of which was the well-known poem by William Ernest Henley.

Out of the night that covers me,
Black as the pit from pole to pole,
I thank whatever gods there be
For my unconquerable soul.

In the fell clutch of circumstance
I have not winced nor cried about.
Beneath the bludgeonings of chance
My head is bloody, but unbowed.

Beyond this space of wrath and tears
Looms but the Horror of the Shade.
And yet the menace of the years
Finds me and shall find me unafraid.

It matters not how straight the gate,
How charged with punishment the scroll,
I am the master of my fate;
I am the captain of my soul.

So in January of 1932, I caught the yellow school bus on the corner near the Shermans and started to high school. Three years

29

and one semester later, I finished at Vaughn, New Mexico. With all my heart I thank Mrs. Sherman for what she could see in me that cold winter day. And also thanks to all the Mrs. Shermans in this world.

At the Sherman farm I cooked, helped with the bath of the lady of the manor, and sometimes drove the nice Buick. Mrs. Sherman would lie down in the back seat, and we would drive as far as Cordell. Once when I thought it would be fun to go faster than usual, I heard from the back seat, "That's fast enough."

Mrs. Sherman didn't get along with many of her neighbors and relatives. I knew she had a daughter in the community from whom she was estranged, but I did not know which neighbors she despised. One evening some sort of community program was to be given, and a neighbor girl from across the road said perhaps they could take me. We were in the kitchen making our plans when Mrs. Sherman called me into the living room. She said, "Get that girl out of here as quick as you can!"

I turned back to the kitchen and whispered, "She is as mad at me as she can be and won't let me go." My friend slipped out the back door.

Each evening we would have family worship. That evening there was a long prayer telling the Lord that "there were just some people you can't get along with." She reminded the Lord that we were living in perilous times. Then it was my turn to read a chapter from the Bible. I said we were ready for the book of James, and since I knew that first chapter from memory, I would give it that way. And give it I did — the entire chapter!

At high school I was a stranger in a strange land. I knew it was best that I lay low because there were many people in the area who would know how old I was. It was not exactly a secret that I was there because the *Sentinel Leader* had published a notice under the heading "New Student Is Welcomed."

Altha Wright is Welcomed by the entire student body and faculty as the first new student to enroll in high school this semester. She comes here from Port. She is the only new student enrolled thus far this semester, but perhaps there will be more later.

Even though we had not lived in Port community for ten years,

Grandfather Wright still owned his farm there and had paid taxes on it for thirty years. Still, no one seemed to know me. Or did they? One man with a large family, whose main interest in life was cockfighting, asked my Uncle Henry one day what business did I have at Port School. I lived with the deathly fear that one day I would be called on the carpet and told I would have to pay tuition, which would be impossible. In those days Oklahoma had no free textbooks. The country was going through one of its many depressions; I don't remember what this one was called, but we did well to buy textbooks.

I started a second semester and made good grades in every subject except math. I never did figure out the mysteries of algebra, so after repeating it a few times, I was mercifully given a passing grade in order to get rid of me. Since it was required that you have two years of math in order to graduate, I took a course in general math in my final year and enjoyed that and made good grades.

No one could ever explain to me why all high school freshmen must face two years of algebra and maybe one of geometry, even if they had no desire to be an engineer. Maybe it is required so that teachers could teach it. Others have said that it teaches discipline. I've even heard that it teaches logic. But I don't think it should be required.

I had a conference in the hall one day with the superintendent, Mr. Welsh. He said, "Mrs. Welsh says you are making top grades in English, and you are failing algebra."

I told him I could see no point in going through the agony of algebra.

He said, "That is neither here nor there; the point is that it is a required subject."

Mrs. Slaughter, in English, had us studying a poem by a seventeen-year-old boy written in 1811. Here are my efforts.

Thanatopsis

Surely the poet's main aim in writing this masterpiece of a poem was to show man the majesty of the grave and to teach him not to fear what we call death.

The setting that he uses is that familiar one, nature. As in nature there are both gladness and sorrow, so in our life that our days are not all glad-

ness, when we are apt to think of "that last sad hour." Then, when we think of death in the terms of funerals, pall bearers and the like, we must turn to nature, get out 'neath the open sky and learn a lesson. There observing all about you the trees, the flowers, you may realize that in a few more days your life will be gone, that in a short time even your resting place will be unknown, and you will be part of the earth.

Of course, this is not our final resting place. One writer before this says, "If ye in this life only have hope you are of all men most miserable."

But this, the earth, the resting place of the body is truly magnificent. When the earth claims you, all the hills, vales, trees, all the beauties of nature are your decoration. Great men of all ages are sharing your destiny. If for any reason none mourn your going, that matters little, for life always goes on just the same and days of mourning are few.

With these thoughts on that sleep which we call death, we should view it calmly and accept it as a great and pleasant event.

Not bad for a high school freshman; not so good for a twenty-two year-old girl who had read everything she could get her hands on for the last ten years. Mrs. Slaughter wrote at the end, "Excellent. I think you have a real talent for writing."

My classmates didn't fare so well on William Cullen Bryant. For on thing, we were asked to memorize the last stanza:

So live, that when thy summons comes to join
The immeasurable caravan, which moves
To that mysterious realm, where each shall take
His chamber in the silent halls of death.
Thou go not, like the quarry slave at night,
Scourged to his dungeon, but, sustained and soothed
By an unfaltering trust, approach thy grave,
Like one who wraps the drapery of his couch
About him, and lies down to pleasant dreams.

At lunchtime my classmates said, "I can't memorize that crazy stuff. It's ridiculous to ask anyone to memorize that! I cannot get it."

Port students hadn't had many dealings with "quarry slaves" or "dungeons." I spoke up and said, "I don't think it is difficult."

A fourteen-year-old girl said, "Well, if I were as old as you are, I wouldn't find it hard to memorize either."

End of discussion.

My biology teacher, Mr. Howell, was dedicated and interesting. My grades were good there. One day a student asked in class, "What is evolution?"

"Well," said Mr. Howell, "that is a big question." He didn't know where to start.

Finally he said, "Do any of you remember the Scopes trial?" Up popped my hand.

Mr. Howell asked, "Is Altha the only one who remembers the Scopes trial?"

I had to think fast, so I said meekly, "I remember my folks talking about it."

Of course, I remembered the Scopes trial! It was reported in all the farm papers. We read about it in the *Semi-Weekly Farm News* and the *Kansas City Star*. I was fifteen years old when William Jennings Bryant died.

I went home to my parents that summer, and then it was decided that I would stay with Aunt Birdie and Uncle Henry for the next school term. They also lived in the Port community.

One day Mr. Welsh called me into the superintendent's office and asked about my being in school there. I told him I was staying with relatives and as far as schooling was concerned, I had no parents. I was censored no further.

Mr. Welsh was the son-in-law of Professor Coffey who was famous as superintendent of Port School even before it became consolidated with many smaller schools in the area. At one time Port School had the distinction of being the largest rural consolidated school in Oklahoma. Students came in twenty buses.

Once before attending as a student, some cousins took me to Port School to visit. Professor Coffey was keeping study hall. When students raised their hands to ask him how to spell a word, he always said, "Ask your Uncle Noah."

The school year of 1933 I stayed in an empty bedroom at cousin Ethel Ward's house. They had three small children. They lived half-way between my folks' home and the school at Port. My room was unheated, but I could sleep there and fix enough to eat to keep going. Every weekend I rode the school bus as far as it went, then walked the rest of the way home. I still have the report card signed by the Wards. The grades were all good, except math.

Then it was decided that in order for me to finish with the 1935 class I would have to get a few credits at summer school. I went to Weatherford, a college town. I enjoyed the large church, the concerts, and getting to know new people. With other neighbor girls, I lived in an old boarding house. We ate mostly waffles made with an old waffle iron. Many teachers from different schools were there for the summer to get credits to keep their teaching certificates in order. I remember my Aunt Ethel's giving me a dollar bill once, saying, "Stick this in your pants pocket." It was stolen by a roommate. A tiny bit of money from my mother's egg and cream sales kept me going.

By then my parents had moved to the Archibald place which was on the school bus route to Lone Wolf High School. So I entered Lone Wolf High.

My half-brother was then living on a claim in Torrance county in New Mexico. He had written me that in New Mexico you could teach in rural schools with a high school diploma if you had one summer of work at the University of New Mexico. I knew that I would be able to teach in a one-room country school. One of my relatives had a school and I was better in English than she was.

I began to see a light at the end of the tunnel.

Home of grandparents John and Elizabeth Wright, 1900 — Port, Oklahoma

Aunt Belle, 1905

Goldie and Charlie Wright, 1909

23

NETTLETON. 8. 7. 8. 7. D.

ROBERT ROBINSON, 1735-1790   JOHN WYETH (?), 1770-1858

1. Come, Thou Fount of ev - ery bless - ing, Tune my heart to sing Thy grace;
2. Here I raise mine Eb - en - e - zer; Hith - er by Thy help I'm come;
3. O to grace how great a debt - or Dai - ly I'm con-strained to be!

Streams of mer - cy, nev - er ceas - ing, Call for songs of loud - est praise.
And I hope, by Thy good pleas - ure, Safe - ly to ar - rive at home.
Let Thy good - ness, like a fet - ter, Bind my wan - dering heart to Thee:

Teach me some me - lo - dious son - net Sung by flam - ing tongues a - bove;
Je - sus sought me when a stran-ger, Wan-d'ring from the fold of God;
Prone to wan - der, Lord, I feel it, Prone to leave the God I love;

Praise the mount! I'm fixed up-on it, Mount of Thy re - deem-ing love.
He, to res - cue me from dan-ger, In - ter-posed His pre-cious blood.
Here's my heart, O take and seal it, Seal it for Thy courts a - bove. A - MEN.

Tune for Cradle Hymn

38

Frontier Church, 1935, near Moriarty, N.M.

From a Grant Wood painting of a country school

Cumiford School House, 1935

Elbert counsels a senior about his test results at is office in Espanola High School, 1948

Loretta (Elledge) helping on a major decision at the Shop, 1970

The Shop on Canyon Road

Chapter 4
LIFE BEGAN IN NEW MEXICO

In 1933 you could file a claim on land in some parts of New Mexico. You had to make certain improvements, live on the land a required length of time, then the land became yours.

My half-brother Ona had filed on land along with several of his relatives, the Rayners. Sam and Vera Ritter were the first of the Rayners to come. Vera was Ona's cousin. Vera's parents, Mate and Butch Babcock followed. Uncle Earl and Aunt Polly Rayner came. Soon their sons joined them. Uncle Guy and Aunt Ethel Rayner came. Grandmother Rayner came. They all filed on land in Torrance and Guadalupe counties. Grandmother Rayner was my father's mother-in-law the first time he married. She was Ona's grandmother.

I was attending Lone Wolf High School when my brother wrote to me about the opportunities of New Mexico. My Uncle Henry and his two sons, who were in their late thirties, had heard of Pie Town in western New Mexico. It was supposed to be the opportunity country for farmers who would like to begin all over again. Oklahoma's small farmers were being "tractored out" and the procession of families with cars loaded down with the necessities of life was soon to begin heading toward California. I cried when I read *The Grapes of Wrath,* and years later when I saw Woody Guthrie's story, "Bound for Glory," because these told my story, too. We didn't cry in those days. We just put one foot in front of the other and kept going.

Uncle Henry said I could tag along with them on a visit to New Mexico. On the way we stopped at Faye Cluck's home in Gruver,

Texas, and she loaned me her nice riding boots and breeches. Then we drove on to my brother's home. He had built a house of rock and it was comfortable. He had a large family who seemed glad to see some Oklahomans. Then my uncle and cousins went on to investigate Pie Town, and I stayed at Ona's. It was all so different. These people were pioneers, I felt.

While I was visiting my brother, I went for a ride on horseback into Vaughn one day. It was March and I got a good sunburn, not knowing that at that altitude the sun was closer. We tied the horses and walked into the stores. There were many Spanish-speaking people around. Some of the buildings were of adobe. This was not a fake set-up for a movie; this was real. I was coming back to the land for my last year of high school.

My uncle and cousins came back from Pie Town, picked me up and we drove back to Oklahoma. There I found that the Lone Wolf School had burned to the ground, but the town had made arrangements for the different classes to meet in churches and lodge buildings, and I finished my junior year there.

In the late summer of 1934, my brother Orville and his friend Woody Sunderland took me to begin life in New Mexico. I was to stay on the ranch with Ona, his wife Julia, and their children: Hazel, Cecil, Doris Elaine, Dorothy, Helen and June. I planned to finish high school at Encino.

Some of the Rayner clan had given up on their dreams and had gone back to northeastern Oklahoma. But Ona and his family stayed, as well as several of his aunts and uncles and Sam and Vera Ritter. Sam and Vera took me under their wing. This was the beginning of a lifelong friendship.

These were hard times for ranchers and small farmers. When Franklin Roosevelt came to the White House as President, the economic structure of the country was tottering. Fear and despair hung over the nation. "We must act quickly," he said. Congress passed a flood of anti-depression measures. We had WPA for the unemployed. We had CCC camps. And we survived. Today prosperous Encino ranchers grow extra fancy sheep and Pendleton buys all the wool.

One program paid farmers to kill their unproductive cows. A

group of us, the Wrights, Rayners, Ritters, and Babcocks gathered at the Babcock barn on the day of a butchering. Everyone helped. I helped skin the cattle. Any meat that would do was taken home and made into hamburger. And the ranchers had a few dollars ahead.

Another way some ranchers managed to get a few dollars was to drive some cattle across the railroad track at train time. If a cow was killed the railroad paid for it.

I entered Encino High for my final year. I took typing, Spanish, general math, and whatever other subjects I needed. I played basketball. The school was small and I loved it. My best friend was Lucille Bigbee. When a grade school teacher became ill, I did substitute teaching for a while.

Sam Ritter drove one of the school buses to gather up the children from the ranches on the east side of Encino. Each bus driver was responsible for his bus and its upkeep. Once toward the end of the school year Sam's bus began to give him trouble, and finally it had to be put in the garage for serious repair. Sam found an old Model T sedan in good running order and at a bargain price. He ran his route and picked up some of the children in his family car. I gathered up the others in the old Model T.

In January Mrs. Seth Howell asked if I would like to come and stay with her. She ran the WPA office in Encino. Mr. Howell was away, tending a ranch in Arizona. My brother had too many mouths to feed, so I accepted.

It would be hard to explain what Encino was like at that time. It would have made a good background for a Western movie. Up the street from us lived a former governor of New Mexico, Richard C. Dillon and his family. He ran one of the Bond Brothers Stores, and Mrs. Dillon helped with the bookkeeping. Bond brothers were well-known sheep men and had several stores. I sometimes walked home from school with the Dillon children, Betty and Malcolm.

When I was going to graduate from high school, I went to Bond's store to buy white shoes for the junior-senior banquet. Dick Dillon came to the shoe department and held up a hundred dollar bill. He said, "How would you like to have this for a graduation present?" Needless to say, he didn't give it to me. Not many hundred dollar bills were seen in those days, so he had to show it to me.

45

One day we were hit with the great dust storm of the Depression. It swept across Oklahoma and Texas, carrying particles of the finest dust, almost black in color. I was riding the bus home when it began. One of the children asked, "Why is Altha crying?" I wasn't crying; the dust made my eyes weep. As I said, you didn't cry in those days.

We tied handkerchiefs over our noses and mouths, and we went to bed wearing them. The next morning the dust had come through all the cracks and the beds were covered with it. It was in our hair, in our scalps. There was no time to shampoo. We went to school, wondering what would happen next.

I spent most weekends with Sam and Vera and their two children, Kenneth and Janiece. One day when Janiece was about eleven, we decided to ride Redbuck. Despite his handsome name, Redbuck had a bad reputation. He didn't want people to ride him. I had been on horses all my life, so I didn't see why this should stop me. So, while no one was looking, we saddled up Redbuck and rode, one at a time. And he gave us very little trouble! It was really more foolhardiness than skill, and maybe the horse knew this and decided to behave.

Church was held in ranch homes once a month. Reverend Young, a Presbyterian, held services in Sam's blacksmith barn, using the anvil for a pulpit. We were supposed to keep things going in between the minister's visits by having Sunday School.

Vera had a piano. Wherever I found a piano, I would sit down and play by ear. One night Sam, Vera, Kenneth, and an itinerant cowboy were sitting at the kitchen table playing cards. I was in the living room trying to pound out "Over the Waves" waltz. The cowboy commented, "You know, that sounds a little bit like "Over the Waves." I still play the piano by ear, and sometimes people recognize the music!

In February the Education Department of the State of New Mexico decided that Encino could not qualify to graduate seven seniors. It had something to do with the number of enrollment. We were told that we would have to go to Vaughn for the months of March and April in order to graduate. So once again I had to find a home where I could attend Vaughn High every day. Finally, a cousin, Lee Wright, and his wife Minnie said I could stay with them. I rode the bus every day.

I graduated from Vaughn High School, along with twenty-one others, on April 26, 1935. Mr. Minire, the superintendent, tried to say something about each graduate as they came forward for that diploma. I was last. "And now, Altha Wright, who has gone to five different high schools."

Mr. Minire didn't know my story. He didn't know my age. He didn't know how many times I had dragged cotton sacks down the row. He didn't know how many families I had lived with, or how many had befriended me. A few months later, I came to Mr. Minire and asked him to send my transcript to Estancia so I could teach. Mr. Minire said, "Let me tell you something, Altha. You go to school, get your degree. Don't fool around with these little two-bit schools."

If only Mr. Minire knew how happy I would be to teach in a "two-bit school!' If not, it was back to Oklahoma for the rest of my life and the battle would be over.

Someone told me that they needed a teacher at Manzano, a Spanish-speaking village in the Manzano mountains. Sam and Vera took me up there. They sat in the front seat, with Janiece and Kenneth and me in the back. Manzano was a small typical town, all low adobe buildings and unpaved streets running this way and that. There was one big general store, and we were to find Mr. Juan Valdez, president of the school board there.

As we walked down the street, we passed two young men, lolling against a sun-baked wall. One made a soft remark and the other laughed loudly. This did not make us feel welcome, and I suggested we go home.

But we went on to the store and found Mr. Valdez. He greeted us, "I am Juan Valdez, of what service can I be to you?"

"I have come to apply for your school, Mr. Valdez. I have my credentials here, and I have been recommended at the superintendent's office at the county seat in Estancia."

He said, "We will go over to the building across the street where we will find the other board members."

We went back to our car and drove across the street. Mr. Valdez and another man hunkered down against the building and had a long discussion. We waited in the car. Mr. Valdez came over to us and said, "We want to ask the lady one question, please."

"Yes, indeed," I said.

"We would like to know if the lady is a Republican or a Democrat. It is necessary."

I was shocked. If I gave the wrong answer, my chance was gone.

"But I've never voted. I've been too young to vote. I couldn't say."

"Just tell us what your folks are."

"My folks? Oh, yes! Sam, what are you?"

Sam roared, "I'm a Democrat."

"That's fine," said Mr. Valdez. "You know we have to go along with the administration in Washington. That's just fine."

I didn't get the Manzano school, but I got one that was easier for me. But that came later.

Many years after this, I was working at the State Oil Conservation Commission in Santa Fe as a file clerk. John Burroughs was governor. I wrote Sam and Vera a letter about my new job. Sam sent a post card right back. "Glad you have a new job, and that it is under the Democrats. I remember when you were converted up on Manzano Mountain."

Chapter 5
SCHOOLTEACHING

After graduating from high school, I made a trip back to Oklahoma. My mother somehow managed to get enough money together for my fee for the summer session at the University of New Mexico. That was about twenty dollars.

My Bethel pastor, Reverend Simms, and Mrs. Simms took me to Foss, Oklahoma, to catch the bus to Albuquerque.

When I arrived in Albuquerque, I took a taxi to the South Edith home of Reverend Simms' sister, Naomi, and her husband Burton Dennis. They had never met me, but kind words from Reverend Simms were my introduction. They took me under their wing and were to be close friends for many years.

Not long after my arrival, Mrs. Cuda, who lived in the next street, invited me to stay with her. She was a widow with a heart of gold. Who says the Lord doesn't take care of his own?

Burton and Naomi Dennis were attending the University, Burton as a student pastor. Each weekend they would go to Moriarty and the Frontier Church, hold services and visit in the homes, then back to Albuquerque for another week of schooling. The young people of Moriarty who were struggling to get through the University would ride home with the Dennises each weekend, spend time with their parents and then ride back with them. The mothers would bake something to help the students get by for another week. My husband says he will never be able to look at another piece of chocolate cake in his lifetime.

While I was taking education courses at the University, I sent

49

out letters applying for a teaching job. One day a letter came, telling me of a school needing a teacher near Mountainair. Its official name was Mesa School, but everyone called it the Cumiford School after the man who had donated the land where it was built.

The Dennises took me down to talk to Mr. Cumiford. He was plowing a field, so Naomi sat in the car while Burton and I climbed over the furrowed ground to meet Mr. Cumiford and make my application. As we talked with him, he seemed very reasonable, and said he would let me know his decisions. In the conversation he said, "I'll tell you one thing, Miss. I don't have any use for that fellow Hughes from Moriarty. He tried to run our schools from the county seat. No-sir-ee, I don't like that fellow." My eyes got big. I said nothing. There was nothing to say, as Mr. Hughes was my friend and had told me about the Cumiford school. Later, a letter came from Mr. Cumiford accepting my application.

One day toward the end of the summer school term in Albuquerque, a car drove up at Mrs. Cuda's. I looked out and decided it had been in a terrible accident. I wondered who had been injured. But it was the Ritter family coming to take me home! Sam had traded for another car. Though it looked a fright, it would run, and I was so glad to see them.

Then began my preparation to move to my school. I went to the bank at Vaughn and borrowed twenty-five dollars, by showing them the letter that I was to teach. My brother, Bob, came from Oklahoma to stay with me and to attend Mountainair High School. Somehow I found a couple of beds. I went to Bond's store and bought supplies. One was a sack of flour. My mother got quilts and other household things together, packed them in a wonderful old trunk, and my father shipped it out to us.

The Ritters loaded everything into the school bus, and we headed for Mountainair and on to the school. Sam and Vera took several young people under their wings during their life time and helped any way they could.

We were told that there was a teacherage across the road from the school where we were to live. As we came in sight, Bob said, "There is the chicken house; wonder where the teacherage is." That was it! We moved in, I curtained off a partition for Bob's bed, the stove went up, and soon everything was comfortable. For a bathroom we went across to one of the school's outhouses.

My salary was fifty dollars a month, plus ten dollars more for the janitor work Bob would do. The salary was in keeping with the times for one-room rural schools. One of my bright students, Fred Cumiford, today makes more than sixty dollars a day. It is in keeping with the times.

Then Mr. Cumiford decided that a good bean harvest was coming up, and that we would delay the opening of the school for a month so the children could help with the bean harvest. He offered me a job helping his daughters cook for the harvest hands.

I don't believe Grant Wood was ever in New Mexico. I'm sure he never saw my little white school house in Torrance County. Yet, after studying in Paris and Munich, he came back to Iowa and began to paint the rural Midwest School houses and harvest hands at work. His "Arbor Days," painted in 1932, is a true-to-life picture of the Cumiford school, with its front steps, outhouses and well with a concrete footing. The rolling hills do not fit in, for it was flat New Mexico farm land. Grand Wood also painted "Dinner for Thrashers" and it, too, is reminiscent of the days we cooked and served the thresher crew during the bean harvest.

One day Mr. Cumiford said I could take his wonderful Buick car and drive up to Estancia to get my supplies for the coming school year.

One of the students who bummed a ride home with Burton and Naomi to Moriarty was Elbert Edgar Earnest. He was in his second year of school at the University of New Mexico. He was also looking for a teaching position and found a four-room school at Cedarvale, some thirty-five miles from me.

He came to see me on Sundays and also helped me with lesson plans. He had two years of college — why shouldn't he? We went to teachers meetings for the county in Estancia. There it was decided to raise the qualifications for teachers. That was the beginning death toll for one-room schools.

Elbert took me to meet his family. They were not overly impressed; nevertheless, we became engaged. We were married December 22, 1935 by Burton Dennis at Frontier Church near

Moriarty.

We had made plans to go to my home in Oklahoma and to have a home wedding there with the Reverend R.E. Smith officiating. Reverend Smith had performed the wedding ceremony for my parents some twenty-six years before. Then an epidemic of spinal meningitis broke out in that state, and our plans were off.

Some nine and one-half months later, James Wright Earnest was born. He must have been the most beautiful baby, the most wanted baby, the most healthy baby that anyone had ever heard about!

Did my pupils have a suspicion that their teacher might be pregnant? Probably not. One morning I had morning sickness but was able to keep teaching that day. In those days there were all sorts of superstitions, and many of them concerned pregnancies. This was a small community and stories spread fast. One morning the "big boys" killed a snake on the way to school. They brought it to school and hung it on a tree. They said, "Miss Wright, come look at the snake we killed." I went out and spent some time admiring the ugly thing, knowing full well that any inkling that the teacher might be pregnant was gone. Those who were pregnant didn't look at such.

I tried to make school interesting. I would read poetry that I thought would have some meaning to them. One day a school supervisor came to check on schools in that part of the country. Thank goodness it was time for seventh and eighth grade geography! I presented the lesson and said, "Luke, go to the board and draw a rough sketch of South America." Luke did that quickly.

"Now, Floyd, put the nations within South America." Floyd filled in the countries with no trouble.

Someone told me recently that schools no longer teach geography. No wonder that the New Mexico magazine has a column every month with tales headed "One of Our Fifty Is Missing."

Many times at the end of the day, I would cross over to the school from the teacherage and play the pump organ for an hour or two. "Amazing Grace" was the song that gave me the most strength.

Through many dangers, toil and snares,
I have already come;
Twas Grace that brought me safe thus far
And Grace will lead me home.

Chapter 6
DEPRESSION AND WAR YEARS

After our schools were over, we returned to Albuquerque, and Elbert went to summer school. For a doctor, I chose Dr. Evelyn Frisbee. I had learned of her work at clinics in northern New Mexico through Reverend Young when we had church services at the Ritter home. She became a wonderful friend, not only through the delivery of Jim, but for many years after that.

When summer was over, we moved to Cedarvale for Elbert to teach another year. At the end of that year, some of the leading citizens decided that there should be a complete house cleaning of all teachers, and all new teachers were hired for the coming year. At that time it seemed unreasonable and unfair, but that decision caused us to move back to Albuquerque where Elbert, after two years, received his Bachelor of Arts in Education. His parents drove over from Estancia to see him graduate with honors as a member of Phi Kappa Phi, a scholastic fraternity. I could not go to his banquet because I did not have the proper clothing.

How did we live during those two years? You must remember that the Great Depression was on. Really, all the depressions were great, but we'll call this the Great-Great Depression. No one had any money. Hamburger was thirty-five cents a pound. Elbert worked at the University half days for about thirty dollars a month. Our Jim went to a WPA nursery school in connection with the University. We tried taking in boarders for a while, but that was not too successful.

Finally, discouraged, one Sunday afternoon I wandered down

on Columbia Street, saw a tiny house behind a larger house and asked if it was for rent. I think the rent was $10.00 a month. We took it and moved in. There are a lot of nice people in this old world. The Sitchlers who let us move into this one-room cottage were one such family. Our furnishings were much like what we had in the teacherage at the Cumiford school. I bought yellow screen curtain material for five cents a yard and made curtains all around. We bathed in a glavanized tub. Next door was the lovely home of the Lawrence Dixons. They helped every way they could and became good friends. They would let us stay in their home while they went on vacations.

One day I saw an ad for part-time housework. That is how we met Ruth and Paul Logan and their son John. I became a "Hazel" for that family, at five dollars a week. Every day at noon I walked to the Logans, did some housework and prepared the evening meal. After clean-up, Elbert would meet me, with Jim riding piggy-back, and we walked home. We walked everywhere we went in those days.

Mr. Logan had come to New Mexico for his health. Mrs. Logan was County Superintendent for Sandoval County and drove to Bernalillo every day.

They had come from a prosperous farm in Indiana. One day there was a financial emergency of some sort, and they had to phone back to Ruth's parents for help. Ruth said, "It wasn't always like this; we used to live on the farm and had plenty." This hadn't been so in my case! I was glad to work for the Logans and escape the farm.

John was a fifteen-year-old high schooler. He could have played Mickey Rooney's part in an Andy Hardy movie. He would bring his compositions for me to read and pronounce judgment on.

During that time I was taking some morning courses at the University. One class was under Julia Kelerher in English. She said I had some writing ability but couldn't spell. I already knew about the spelling.

In 1939 Elbert accepted a teaching position at Vaughn. He was qualified to teach high school math, Spanish, and most any high school subject. But for some reason, teachers were a dime a dozen, and he was given fifth and sixth grades. So here I was back at Vaughn, with Mr. Minire as school superintendent. This is the same

Mr. Minire that some four years before had advised me not to fool around with little two-bit schools. Well, here I was, with a son and a husband with a degree.

The salary was about ninety dollars a month. We were once more in a two-room house, but the rent was low. We invested in a second-hand car. Our neighbors were the Doughertys who became lifelong friends. Jim wasn't old enough to go to school, but he sometimes visited school with Margaret Dougherty. As school closed, everyone got a report card except Jim. So we got out cardboard and invented a report card for him.

As soon as the school term was over, we gathered up Bernice, Elbert's little sister, and went to see the kin folk. We visited my parents in Oklahoma, then on to the Ritters in Wyandotte, then on down to see Elbert's grandfather Maggard in Whiteboro. We also visited all sorts of aunts, uncles, and cousins. This started a tradition that lasted for years — going to Oklahoma to visit the kin folks every summer as soon as school was out.

As the second year of school of Vaughn was coming to an end, I decided it was time to take care of an old problem. Elbert was born with ptosis of one eyelid, sometimes called a "lazy eye." His grandmother Earnest had the same defect. Elbert had been teased at grade school and called "old one eye" until he had built up a wall to where he did not discuss it with anyone. The eye was preventing him from getting a better job in a bigger school.

For instance, after graduation from UNM with top honors and the best recommendation from his professors, he began applying for positions. He thought he had the job at a school in northeastern New Mexico, when the superintendent refused him. He told one professor that the reason was that eye. For the first time, we discussed the problem.

I marched downtown and told Dr. Frisbee our troubles. She said, "There is a young doctor that has moved to Santa Fe. He has just graduated and he and his wife have one youngster, as you have. I'll talk to him and tell him you are worthy people."

She did talk to Dr. Eggenhoffer and wrote to me about it. As the second term at Vaughn ended, I made arrangements for the operation. We knew Elbert's family would be opposed to this. They said he could see out of that eye; leave it alone.

When school was out, we headed for Santa Fe. But first we had to visit Elbert's parents on a ranch near Moriarty. Grandmother Earnest asked Jim, "Jim, what are you going to do when school is out?"

Jim, about four years old, said, "We're going up to Santa Fe to have Daddy's eye fixed." We hadn't thought to warn Jim not to tell of our plans. Now they knew; they did not approve.

The operation was a wonderful success, and I fell in love with Santa Fe.

In 1941 a better position opened at Hot Springs, New Mexico, so we moved there. (It is now called Truth or Consequences, or "T or C.") Hot Springs was a well-known health resort. The baths were supposed to cure whatever ailed you.

Our son, Stephen, was born there in 1942. By then World War II was cooking up. I had started prenatal care under an M.D., but he was drafted and had no choice but to leave. I then found Dr. Maloney, an osteopath.

After Stephen was born, I went in for a post-natal checkup. Dr. Maloney called Elbert aside and asked if he would like to make fifteen dollars. Would he spend the night with Jim White? Jim White had discovered Carlsbad Caverns and was still one of the superintendents there. He had a drinking problem and came once a year to Hot Springs to dry out. A nurse friend had stayed with him, and we had heard tales of his climbing the walls and other horrors. Elbert, not having experience along that line, refused.

As the school term ended, school teachers hunted for summer jobs. Elbert applied at Carrie Tingley Hospital, but received no answer. He went to Albuquerque and applied at Bell Trading Post. They wanted him for a shipping clerk because of his beautiful handwriting. He then went over to Madrid to apply for a job as payroll clerk. Both jobs did not work out, as they did not want to hire someone for only summer work. Back at Hot Springs the Carrie Tingley Hospital job came through, and he began working on the grounds.

Then they asked him to take a van load of crippled children into northern New Mexico, deliver them to their homes, and pick up another van load of cripled children to bring back to Carrie Tingley for treatment. About that time Stephen decided to enter into this world. Fortunately, I had a wonderful neighbor, Mrs. Wagner, who cared for me, Stephen, and young Jim while Elbert was up north. Mrs. Wagner today is ninety-five and lives in Santa Fe, and we sometimes get together and talk about the old days in Hot Springs.

Jim entered first grade that year, and by then the war was in full swing. School teachers with families were advised to enter war work, since, at that time, they were not likely to be drafted. So in November we left for California. We had friends in a housing project near El Sereno and had some things shipped there.

I, who had never seen a city larger than Albuquerque, then probably less than 50,000, was suddenly living in Los Angeles. I lived in an apartment with Jim and four-month-old Stephen, while Elbert worked the swing shift or graveyard shift at Lockheed. Gas was rationed, as was food, clothes, and almost everything else. In the car pool that Elbert rode in, he was often asked to drive back home at night, as all the others were too drunk to drive. There was crime on every hand. Across the street from us, a young father committed suicide. Next door to us, a woman lived with her teen-aged son. She had an affair with a married man and had a baby. She kept working and left the baby in its crib all day and had a teen-ager across the street to look in on this baby occasionally. Once, the married man and his wife came to see the baby. None of this was ever reported to any authority. At the same time, there was a story in the paper about a horse that had been left tied out in the rain. The owner was arrested for this.

I had no choice but to live there. Housing was impossible to find. David was born in 1944 in Alhambra, at the White Memorial Hospital, by the Cudal method. I had the best of care. My mother came to care for eighteen-month-old Stephen. The day David was born, Elbert received notice that he would be drafted. Somehow nothing ever came of it.

So I fought the battle with two babies and Jim. Jim was teased on the way to school and on the way home. Stephen ate out of the garbage can. Women fought over the clothes lines. I was frightened most of the time. Elbert was trying all this time to find a house so we could move.

Elbert's sister, Bernice, had developed rheumatic fever in New Mexico. A doctor said she most move to a lower climate, so the entire Earnest family moved to Los Angeles. They stayed with us until they found a house near the Huntington Park area. When David was a few months old, our dream came true. We found a house in the San Fernando Valley and moved there. After about a year, we knew that the war was coming to an end. Schools everywhere were crying for teachers as some teachers had been war casualties, while others went into different work.

One Sunday we went to visit the senior Earnests. Elbert told them that he had received permission from his draft board in Santa Rosa, New Mexico, and from the War Draft Board to return to teaching. "So we are going home," he told them.

"Going home," they said. "What do you mean, going home?"

They felt they had reached Beulah Land in Los Angeles. We felt we would be glad to get back to the Land of Manana.

Chapter 7
AFTER THE WAR

We lived in Cedar Crest that summer, 1945. The Dixon family of Albuquerque let us have their mountain cabin.

Next Elbert decided to teach in Espanola in the high school. There was a shortage of housing, but a committee was formed to find housing for the new teachers. We went to church at McCurdy Mission, and the children went there for their schooling. Elbert belonged to Toastmasters and Kiwanis Club.

We built a small house after purchasing a few acres of land. We had a cow and chickens. Orchards were everywhere, and I canned hundreds of jars of fruit. We picked apples off the ground for free and turned them into applesauce. Stephen said his arm was permanently crooked from having to turn the mill for applesauce.

One of our neighbors was Dorothy Thomas who wrote short stories for *McCalls, Saturday Evening Post,* and other popular magazines. Other friends were General Corlett and his wife, who had a lovely ranchito. Mrs. Corlett was a charming hostess, and they both helped make Espanola an interesting place to live.

Sam and Isabel Ziegler also became neighbors. Kathleen and I used to sit in the doctor's waiting room with Georgia O'Keeffe who also waited patiently. She loved to talk with children. Her voice was very low, almost like a man's. She was a patient of Dr. Sam Ziegler then, and he was her doctor for more than thirty years, until she moved to Santa Fe a few years before she died in 1986.

One day while I was sitting in the waiting room, the nurse walked through and in passing said to one of my friends — "Your urine is beautiful, just beautiful." My friend turned bright red! She wasn't used to having her urine discussed in public.

Our daughter Kathleen was born November 11, 1948, at the Espanola hospital with Dr. Sam Ziegler delivering her. There was great rejoicing that at last the Earnests had a girl. There were gifts and flowers. We sent a telegram to the grandparents in Los Angeles.

When Kathleen was a baby, Elbert went to the summer term at the University of New Mexico and earned his Master's degree. Jim was man of the house that summer, though he was only thirteen years old.

When Stephen and David were Cub Scouts, I became a den mother. I somehow kept the household going and found time to work with that lively group. We made a full-sized tent out of unbleached muslin. The Cubs decorated it with scout symbols and tried to follow the manual.

One evening we put on a program at McCurdy auditorium. We practiced a skit to entertain the parents. On stage, we had a table, a large bottle of elixir and a spoon, with Dr. Feelgood sitting there ready to cure any and all ailments. One Cub Scout, whom I'll call Edward, was elected to be the first patient. Edward's mother was sitting in the audience, about eight and one-half months pregnant.

We had dressed an open umbrella with a skirt, made a head, painted the face, put a lady's hat on top. Edward was to say, "Doctor, I'm too fat, I want to reduce." Dr. Feelgood was supposed to reply, "I have just the thing for you," and then administer a big spoonful of the medicine. Edward was then supposed to gently let down the umbrella and instantly become slender.

Edward came in and said, "Doctor, I'm too fat. I want to *produce.*"

The house roared and people glanced at Edward's mother to see if she would like to produce.

There was a women's club in Espanola, and we had some very fine programs. Mrs. Bond came and gave a paper on Steinbeck, with a brief review on "Of Mice and Men." Another time she talked on Bach and played a few records of his music. Mary Sweet, a high school teacher, gave a review of Jesse Stuart. One time the program was to be Exiolda Trujillo playing her very best piano recital piece and a teacher from Santa Clara telling of her trip to Europe. The dear lady from Santa Clara came first, and she began, "It was a beautiful and clear day as we left . . ." Then she continued, and she continued, and continued. Mr. Trujillo, who had come to hear his daughter play, became restless, not to mention the rest of us. The club president tried to stop her, saying we had limited time. The teacher would respond, "I'll be finished soon," and would continue some more. Finally, we had our piano solo and everyone went home late.

Agnes Morley Cleaveland was once a speaker at Espanola. She wrote *No Life for a Lady*, the story of her life in western New Mexico. Her book has been popular for over forty-five years.

Our children took piano lessons from Phyllis Snow, wife of Dr. Robert Snow. Phyllis would give a recital, and all the parents would try to be present. I have a photo made in 1950 of Mrs. Snow and her pupils, who were: Foster Stringfield, Jim Earnest holding Kathleen Earnest, Monte Aker, Charles Barbee, Steve Earnest, David Earnest, Carol Schutchel, Sammy Ziegler, Norman Ziegler, and Larry Aker.

When we came to Espanola, the high school did not have a yearbook. Elbert soon had his pupils working on that, and the first one came out that spring. Elbert also saw the need of a youth organization for the community and helped get that started.

After ten years at Espanola, we decided to move to Santa Fe. First, there was the business of selling our Espanola property and finding a house in Santa Fe. I would load the little ones in the car and go look at houses. After many trips, we found a gem of a house built by architects Cordner and Steinbach. It was to have been the Cordner's home for the rest of their lives. But after several years, they had to move to a lower climate for health reasons. We moved in time to enroll everyone in school. Jim was then college age.

Elbert began his career as an insurance agent, and opened his office in the Spitz building at 54 1/2 West San Francisco Street. He was to be at that location for more than thirty years. I began working at Spitz Jewelry.

Jim began working for the State Book Depository where former governor John Miles was director. Jim and later Stephen worked at the Book Depository for several years. Stephen was a friend of Jimmy Miles and spent many happy hours at the Miles Ranch south of

Santa Fe. There he became quite a horseman and has a nice collection of ribbons won at gymkhanas.

Jim decided after a year at the University of New Mexico that he wanted to go to school at Otterbein in Westerville, Ohio. Some of the wonderful people he had met at McCurdy helped with the decision.

At Otterbein, Jim wrote us that he had found the girl he wanted to marry. Barbara Noble had lived near Westerville all her life and so had her grandparents, aunts, and uncles.

He brought her home to see his family as soon as summer vacation began. The moment she walked into our house she said, "I see you have a Western style house."

Before they left Otterbein, her friends had given her a little party, and they all said, "I suppose you will go to see Jim's grandfather." Barbara said, "Oh, yes."

Jim had entered Otterbein with his best pal from Espanola, Alfonso Duran. They pledged the same fraternity and roomed together. They had the room decorated in the best Western motif, a pair of deer antlers on the wall and some scenes of New Mexico. One picture was of an Indian Chief; I believe he was known as "Chief Yellow Horse." Jim's fraternity brothers liked to call Jim "Tex," and if a western came on television, they would yell upstairs for Jim to come see it.

When Otterbein had their Parents' Day, they had each and every building shining clean and all ready for parents who were deciding just where to send their youngsters. When they came to Jim and Alfonso's room, they added a little human interest to their story. "Now this room is for two young men from New Mexico. They come from Espanola where the United Brethren have a school and hospital. Mr. Duran is from a Spanish speaking family and this is Jim's grandfather," pointing to Chief Yellow Horse. Somehow the story grew and when Barbara was coming west, she assured her friends that she would meet Jim's "grandfather."

I began working at the State Oil Conservation Commission as a file clerk. I had not done that sort of work, and everyone was patient in helping me. I was there some five years. One year they decided that I should be at the reception desk, since I talked "Texan.' Most of our out-of-state callers were from oil-rich Texas. Often calls would come in for our supervisor, Ralph Trujillo. They would pronounce his name as "True-jill-o," as in Jack and Jill. His secretary would go down the hall calling for "Mr. True-jill-o," trying to locate him. If I were to suggest that they probably meant "Mr. Tru-hee-o," which was the correct Spanish pronunciation, they would say, "No, Mr. True-jill-o, Mr. True-jill-o!"

After I left the Oil Commission, I tried opening a little shop and sewing all that was sold. It had been a dream for a long time. While working at the Oil Commission, I would go home at five o'clock, then Mrs. Scheuer would close her shop, La Tienda, come by my house and leave everything that needed altering for that day. I would do the alterations that evening, and next morning Elbert would deliver them to La Tienda on his way to work. I also did alterations for Irma's. And I sometimes did sewing at home. One customer I remember was Laura Gilpin, the well known photographer and writer. Miss Foster, the nurse who helped Miss Gilpin for years on the Navajo reservation, was with Miss Gilpin one day. I had some artificial lilies in our living room. Miss Foster got up to smell them, and we laughed when she discovered the lilies were plastic.

Julia Seton, wife of Ernest Thompson Seton, opened a shop at Seton Village in the sixties. I put handmade clothing in her shop. But I, like many, dreamed of opening a little shop of my own. Most people dream of how they would decorate, make a place attractive, what color scheme. But there is a more practical side, like money, location, and knowing what your public wants. I found a location on the enclosed porch of the old Levi Hughes house on Washington Street. We scrubbed and scoured for days. I made lovely drapes, bought mirrors, and soon had a goodly number of customers.

The Bank of Santa Fe was in the rest of the building. Mr. Jack Hester was president. He was a banker in Mountainair in his younger days. We would talk about the depression days when I taught near there.

But things didn't stay happy for the Bank of Santa Fe moved to their new building and a radio station moved in and let it be known that they wanted me out. They played loud hillbilly music and were rude. John Burroughs was in charge of the building so I appealed to him. I have a letter from former Governor Burroughs saying I would stay there but the radio people laughed at that, so I moved out.

I had hardly settled down at home, when Dr. Robert Snow came to visit me one day. He wanted me for his receptionist, secretary, Girl Friday, and office manager. I had known Dr. Snow for many years at Espanola, and Mrs. Snow was the piano teacher for our three sons. I said, "I can't do that; I can't even keep a checkbook." We argued for some time. He wouldn't take no for an answer.

So I began two years with Dr. Snow. Dell Griego was the registered nurse there and she was a Rock of Gibraltar. She said she would help me and she did. Soon after I began to work at Dr. Snow's, he handed me a list of the babies that had been delivered in the last several days. I was to record them. One side of the list was the mother's name, the date of delivery and then the signs for male and female. I told them I didn't know what they meant. They laughed and said, "Don't you ever watch television?" I had to admit I wasn't much of a television watcher.

Our son Stephen, who was in college in Grand Junction, Colorado, phoned us one night that he was married. Mothers and fathers go through such things! He and Susan Banks of Grand Junction were married, and they were coming to Santa Fe. He was nineteen years old. When their son Jeffrey was born, Dr. Snow was the doctor. Susan was diabetic, and had been since she was nine years old. She was also a victim of polio and needed special care. With Dr. McGoy as the doctor who had charge of her diabetes, Dr. Snow was her obstetrician and Dr. Monahan, who was to care for the baby, they decided to take the baby early. They x-rayed the knee of the fetus to see if this was the thing to do.

So, with Dr. Snow doing a cesarian, Dr. McGoy and Dr. Monahan standing outside the door, the nuns watching carefully, Jeffrey was delivered at St. Vincent Hospital. I talked to Dr. Snow afterward. He said there was not to be another pregnancy. I said, "With all the new things in the medical world, that shouldn't be so final."

Dr. Snow said, "I said there is not to be any more pregnancies."

Dr. Snow did not take welfare patients unless there was a difficulty that required a specialist. We had one unmarried welfare patient that came often with her various pregnancies. One day she appeared in an Italian knit suit and a coat with a mink collar. It was my job to find the folder for each patient and take them back to Dr. Snow. I wrote a little note on this one. "They toil not, they spin not, but I say unto you, that Solomon in all his glory was not arrayed like one of these." Luke 12:27.

You have to have a sense of humor. If Dr. Snow forgot to pay us, I would say, "Well, Dr. Snow, I guess Dell and I will eat at La Fonda today and charge it to you since we haven't been paid." He would smile, apologize, and write our checks.

Sometimes things got so hectic that Dr. Snow could not get the paperwork done. All doctors must sit in the hospital and fill out countless forms. When Dr. Snow got behind, Sister Joaquin would phone me and say, "Dr. Snow cannot deliver any more babies until that paperwork is done."

We had so many lovely persons as patients, and there were heart-breaking cases as well. I felt I had the equivalent of a college education in those two years.

Chapter 8
I OPEN THE BIRDWATCHER

It was 1966. Kathleen graduated from high school in the upper ten percent of her class and got a summer job at a gallery on Canyon Road. David went to Viet Nam, Jim was working for J. Edgar Hoover, Stephen was an architect, and Elbert was a successful insurance agent. I began to look around for a location for a dress shop, this time on Canyon Road.

Canyon Road is a narrow crooked road which begins at the edge of the downtown area and meanders upwards towards the foothills of the Sangre de Cristo mountains. It roughly follows the Santa Fe River and ends at the reservoir which supplies the city with water. The lower end is lined with a variety of private homes, shops, galleries, and restaurants, ancient trees and very old buildings.

There was a compound adjoining the historic Borrego House which was the home of Three Cities of Spain, a coffee house. Agnes Sims, a local artist, owned it. It was well-kept, with roses and hollyhocks galore. Every year an outdoor stage in the center was the scene of a Fiesta program. On a beautiful summer night every possible seat was taken, and the spirit of old Santa Fe was reflected in the mariachi music and in the beauty of the Fiesta queen and princesses.

Inside this compound I found one room for my shop. Friends who ran a restaurant and art gallery there moved out so that I could have an affordable place.

We named it the Birdwatcher Shop.

I opened with a few cream cotton, smock-style dresses, a few shirt style dresses for older women, and some pillows. I did not know just what to expect. I agreed with the song "The Times They Are A-Changin'," and that people were hungry for casual clothing. I knew I was in the right place at the right time, but wasn't sure how to handle the opportunity.

One of my best sellers was my smock dress. It was usually made of soft cream cotton or Osnaberg, which we called "Polish silk." Across the yoke was a strip of Austrian braid with decorative stitching around the braid, on the pockets and on the cuffs of the long sleeves. These were made in children's sizes also. I sold one to a teenage girl and years later she was married in this same dress in Germany. Her mother, who played in the Santa Fe Opera orchestra, told me about it.

One of my early customers who wore my smocks was Mary Lou Aswell. She was fiction editor for *Harper's Bazaar* and was a passionate advocate for young writers. She lived in another Canyon Road compound owned by Agnes Sims until her death in 1986. Eudora Welty came to visit her there every year.

Another of my nicest customers was Dorothy Swartz of Colorado. She bought dresses for her little girls. She remained my customer for the seventeen years that the Birdwatcher was on Canyon Road.

I sent one of these smocks to Kathleen at Otterbein College. The girls in the dormitory said, "Kathleen got a package from home. One of the things is a nightgown!" Hippie days and casual clothes had not come to Otterbein!

At the time, it seemed that Santa Fe was a haven for every unconventional soul in our nation. In one of the apartments in the compound lived Sarah Kitchen. She came from a well-to-do family in New England and lived on money her brother sent her each month. She was in her 70's and had spent her entire life proving that she was a rebel. Her small apartment was a hangout for every hippie who could get crammed into it. At night when she had to go to the bathroom, she stumbled over bedrolls on the floor. In the daytime they lolled in the compound. There was shoplifting, stealing, and rudeness.

I phoned Agnes Sims, the landlady. "I don't know what can be done," she said. "They are hanging on the fence around my place like black birds."

Sarah would sometimes phone the parents of some of the more pitiful of her friends. All they could offer was, "We can send you some money to help feed them."

By the second year, the store on the street became empty, and Miss Sims offered that to me. Sarah moved on and life in general became less hectic.

New Mexico became famous for its hippie communes — the Hog Farm, San Luis, New Buffalo, Placitas, Lama Foundation.

One day that first August at the Birdwatcher, Kathleen and I left the shop and drove out to Tesuque to an estate sale. Kathleen bought a large antique trunk and a few other goodies. When we drove back to Canyon Road, we saw a large old school bus decorated with every color, every design imaginable, at the corner of Canyon Road and Camino del Monte Sol. It had tried to turn around but was too long for the narrow streets. A crowd gathered to see the monstrosity of a bus and the hippies. We had to park near the crowd and decided to carry the trunk to my shop. Kathleen in a very short smock and I in a caftan soon attracted our own spectators. They thought we were part of the bus people and made loud remarks about hippies.

What happened to the trunk? It was lovingly restored and has a home with my cousin in Oklahoma City.

That fall, Kathleen and Monte Corwin wrote from Otterbein that they were planning to be married at Santa Fe at Christmas time. I made Kathleen's wedding dress, my dress, and arranged for the guests. All our family was there for the wedding except David. He called long distance from Viet Nam the day of the wedding.

The ceremony was at the Methodist Church. Five-year-old Jeffrey was ringbearer. At the last day before the wedding, Jim phoned us from Houston that they were coming, with one-month-old James Franklin. My sister Grace and her two daughters Marylin and Carolyn were in the wedding as attendants.

When draft time came for Monte, he decided to take the conscientious objector's route. He and Kathleen moved to Canada. We sincerely thought we might never see them again. We knew if Monte crossed the border to the United States he would be arrested. Monte went to school and received his degree from Waterloo

University. After several years, the United States let those who were conscientious objectors come back into this country. But Monte and Kathleen had become Canadians by then.

David was in Viet Nam for about three years. We kept him in our hearts all that time, but we were not like some of our friends who wrote to their sons every day and spent the rest of the time weeping. David carried a key to our house all those three years. Once when we knew a furlough might be coming up, we had gone to Albuquerque for the day. As we arrived home and unlocked the door, we saw the cameras and luggage in the hallway and my husband said, "Our boy is home."

Only our Lord can understand what three years in Viet Nam can do to a young man as sensitive as David.

Life alternated between the family and the Birdwatcher. The children began having grandchildren, and as they grew up, they all helped in the shop. Even Elbert helped after working at his insurance business all day.

Our first grandchild was Susan Bernice, carrot-top daughter of Jim and Barbara. Later they had Mary Kathleen and James Franklin, whom we all called "Young Jim."

In 1964 Michael James was adopted by Stephen and Susan. I would every adoption was as successful as his. He has been our son and grandson for some twenty-two years, nice-looking and not afraid of hard work.

In November of 1984, we went to Albuquerque to attend the wedding of Jeffrey to Nancy. We were at the hospital when Jeffrey was born. We would take him on trips with us to visit both of his great-grand parents. We took him to Disney Land. He would come spend a week with us and help at my shop. We went to his high school graduation at Villa School in Arizona. Once when I was telling him that the poem "Invictus" had helped me over the rough places, he said, "Mam-maw, I memorized that two or three years ago." We feel he lives every word of that poem.

In August 1970 Kathleen and Monte had twin boys, Jessee Elliott and Guthrie Alan. After the twins were born, it was discovered that Kathleen had multiple sclerosis. She has always had good care under Canada's medical program, and they do not have to worry about the cost. During her strong periods, the Canadians always helped her find the right job.

Pretty soon the grandchildren will be having children!

When Susan was a baby, Jim and Barbara decided to spend the summer with us in Santa Fe. We met them at the airport. Somehow when that huge plane landed, and Barbara began walking to the station where we waited, I became emotional and burst out crying. So did Susan. She didn't know what it was all about, but it seemed the proper thing to do. The people around thought we were rather odd.

In the spring of 1985, Susan graduated from Irvine College in California. I wrote her I didn't think I would come; I might become emotional again.

When young Jim was five or six, they put him on the plane and let him fly alone from Houston to spend a week with us. While Elbert collected his luggage, I visited with Jim. His father had bought a Bentley while they were living in London and had it shipped back to the U.S. with their other goods. I asked young Jim about the Bentley.

"We sold the Bentley."

"You did! That's a shame!"

"When I get big I'm going to move to England."

"And buy a Bentley?"

"Yeah. And if my wife would go away and we didn't have any babies, I'd have the Bentley to keep me company."

Soon, a routine for the Birdwatcher became established. We tried keeping the shop open during January and February but found it was not profitable. So we closed the shop and spent those two months getting ready for ten months of tourists and Santa Fe people.

I designed all the clothes and made the patterns. The fun part was shopping for fabric. If we went visiting somewhere, I looked for the fabric stores. I knew the best stores in Albuquerque, Portales, where my sister Grace lived, and even in San Francisco. Of course this was in addition to helping support Santa Fe stores.

I started out making all the clothes myself and had my Bernina sewing machine set up in the shop in front of a window. Soon I had to find seamstresses to help me. I cut everything out at night or on weekends and parcelled out skirts, dresses, blouses, smocks, jumpers, or ponchos to the women who were especially good at making one thing or another.

Business was good and became even better when I moved into two rooms facing the street. More room and more people added more responsibility. I supplied one of many of Santa Fe's cottage industries. A few things from India and Mexico filled up the racks. We also had hand-woven Pueblo rain dance belts and concho belts.

My clothes were made of cotton, wool, velvet, velveteen, calico, and leather. I often dyed the fabrics to get the soft Southwestern colors I wanted. The Navajo style velvet and velveteen blouses were trimmed with real silver buttons, often made from dimes, or nuggets of real turquoise. They were elegant. Ribbon shirts were a specialty. They were usually calico, but could be plain, and were made after the Plains Indian style, trimmed with lots of colored ribbons which fluttered as you walked. Both Indian styles had matching three tiered gathered skirts, hemmed at the right length to show off boots or moccasins.

The smock was still very popular. The girls from Santa Fe Prep School asked me to make them shorter until they looked like a hospital gown. The rebellion was in full swing, and couples were choosing to be married on a mountain top or in a beautiful meadow. Brides didn't want a wedding gown of satin and pearls, a train and flowers from the florist. Grooms would often wear a cotton shirt with embroidered yoke. Many lovely weddings were held in a meadow, the bride in a Birdwatcher dress, sometimes barefoot, with a bunch of wild flowers for a bouquet.

I was one step ahead of a California designer in providing dresses for these weddings. I made a dress of soft, cream muslin, leg o'mutton sleeves, high Victorian collar, with lots of cream lace. Some two years later, a pattern came out in the pattern books similiar to this.

There was one bride-to-be that I'll always remember. She was from Texas and when she saw the cream muslin dress, she could hardly believe her eyes! I suggested she try it on. She loved it! About that time her mother came in and said, "How quaint."

When the mother left I said, "It is your wedding — can't you wear what you want?"

"You don't understand, My father is a florist."

I did understand. She would walk up the aisle in satin and train and several hundred dollars worth of advertisements for her father's business.

About this time, Hal Wallace came to Santa Fe to make the movie *Red Sky at Morning*, from the book by Richard Bradford. Mr. Wallace's wife, Martha Hyer, came in to buy my clothes. The daughter of author Conrad Richter was another one of my customers. All of these customers were important individuals to me. Many became friends, more than custormers.

But not the people who came in bus tours!

Bus tour ladies never bought anything. They didn't have time to try anything on because the driver only allowed them fifteen minutes. They called to each other:

"Mary Belle, come here. I wish you would come here!"

"What?"

"What does this remind you of? Don't you know? That dress I made by Nadine's pattern. The same material. Don't you remember? Exactly the same."

"Well, I'll be."

"Well, I'll say."

"Oh, my word."

"Well, I'll declare."

"Is that right?"

"Well, I swan."

"Look, Osnaberg, I have curtains made of that."

In the summertime the Baptists from Glorieta found us. One young lady asked, "Are there any lyots in here?"

We asked her to repeat the question once more. She said, "Are there any lyots in here?"

We looked puzzled.

Finally she said, "Oh, never mind; it's sort of dark in here."

One day three ladies came in from Glorieta asking for embroidered blouses and straw bags. They insisted on straw shopping bags. I tried to tell them they were in *New* Mexico, not Old Mexico, but they could not believe me.

Parking has always been a problem on Canyon Road, and still is. One time a car was parked in front of the shop for a week. We couldn't get the police to move it, so we called the second week and told them, "There is a note in the front seat, and we think it may be a suicide note." They towed it away.

Another time a large flatbed truck with a house built on it parked in front of the window. It was complete with a back porch, a broom, the works. It blocked out all our light. The police wouldn't remove it because it was parked legally. Finally it moved.

The Birdwatcher had a Dutch door. The top opened, the bottom closed. Most people could not figure it out. Some crawled over. Most looked helpless as to how to get inside. One summer day at the height of the tourist season, the Birdwatcher had its half door open. Some tourists poked their heads in the door and saw the Birdwatcher clothes. "Oh, we don't need to go in here. This is indigenous clothing."

I commissioned Mary Lou Cook to paint "Birdwatcher Casual Clothes" on the wall near the door and to make another sign. People liked those signs. Five of them were stolen, some of which had to be pried from the walls. Most of the time we felt there was nothing the police could do to recover them, that it was something we had to accept. The last sign stolen had been expensive, and we had spent a goodly amount on the ironwork hanger. When it disappeared, we called the police and claimed a value of two hundred fifty dollars. Within a few days, the sign appeared near Gormley's store up the street. Friends spied it and brought it back. We felt the police had let it be known that this was more than petty crime.

We had folding shutters over our large window facing the street. They had one bullet hole in them. Every night we closed the shutters and opened them each morning. I commissioned Phoebe Hummel to paint them with flowers and birds in the Santa Fe style, still used at La Fonda. These shutters were painted over when the building was sold in 1981.

For help I had every kind of person you can imagine. Some stayed with me through thick and thin. They could throw out a drunk; they could even handle a bus tour! They could take over when we went on vacation or to visit relatives. For example, when Jim and Barbara were living in London with their children, they invited us to meet them in Spain at Malaga for a week of sightseeing. Then we all went on for a week in London. My helpers at the shop kept things running smoothly.

Phoebe Hummel became invaluable help. She was living in Las Vegas, but would come over for two or three days, sometimes sleeping in the back of the shop. When we had a special order for a dress, and I would be ready to throw up my hands in despair, Phoebe would say, "Now, there must be a way to make that fabric hang right." She never gave up, and her optimisim I have learned to treasure from those trying days until now. She now works with her husband, Dr. Paul Hummel, and uses her common sense and optimistic outlook every day.

I found one of my helpers at Dendahls. She was petite, had a beautiful English accent, and could sew beautifully. Nicole and I would have interesting discussions. One day she came back at me and said, "Well, yes, but you believe like that because you are a Christian." That is about the greatest compliment I ever had. I have no idea what we were talking about. I believe it had to do with some of my daily life, not some minor detail about church doctrine.

One night we were watching TV and listening to Dr. Jacob Bronowski begin his series of discussion on his book, *The Ascent of Man.* He was on PBS every Tuesday night for several weeks. It finally dawned on me that he was Nicole's father. I had met her mother and father and sisters, but did not know that she was the daughter of this great man. When Nicole and Jay Plett were married, Nicole wore a lavender calico print dress made Birdwatcher style. The music, food, clothes, and all were in keeping with the times.

After a few years Nicole and Jay decided to adopt a baby. Adoption people ask for letters of recommendation for prospective parents, and Nicole asked if we would write one. We still have a copy of the one we wrote. My husband told Nicole and Jay that they certainly had a lot to live up to if they could see that letter. Another letter they asked for was from Dr. Jonas Salk. Dr. Bronowski was working with Dr. Salk at Salk Institute at La Jolla, California. Dr.

Salk didn't waste time on a letter. He called the adoption agency and said, "This is Dr. Jonas Salk." Of course, the Pletts got a baby and then another baby. Nicole's father died a few years after this, and Dr. Salk did all he could to help through that trying time. Nicole still "lives on the land" and sometimes writes for the art section of the *New Mexican* in Santa Fe.

Barbara Holloway, a weaver, put some of her hand-crafted clothes in the Birdwatcher. She also did some sewing for me.

Elaine Messer began helping in 1978 or 1980 and stayed with me until the end. There was a time when she and her husband spent four years in Kayenta on the Navajo reservation as missionaries, but then they came back for a while, until they went for a summer in Alaska. After each of their safaries, she was anxious to get back to the Birdwatcher and its routine.

Jim and Barbara moved to Santa Fe for a while. Susan and Mary Kathleen helped in the shop. When Jim's job took him to Saudi Arabia, Mary Kathleen stayed with us. I depended on her as shop helper and companion for several years. We cried together, we laughed together, we dreamed together.

One summer day when things were slow, I suggested Mary Kathleen count the people who passed the window wearing a sweater with horizontal stripes. I would give her a nickel apiece.

In a short time she had collected $2.25. There people were not interested in Southwestern styles — only in Southwestern sunshine.

One hot day as Jim and Barbara were getting ready for the move, they found young Jim wrapped up in a wool blanket.

"Jim, what on earth?"

"I'm getting ready to move to Saudi. It's very hot there."

Another summer Jeffrey lived with us, and I put him to work washing the big front window. A little boy studied him for a while and asked, "Are you Mrs. Earnest's maid?"

I made a blue velvet Navajo shirt for Frank Patania, the famous jeweler, while he was living in Arizona. When his check came, we read the memo: "It's beautiful!" Such little things as that often made our day, after a long, hard day.

Katherine Ross always bought Navajo skirts from me if she was in Santa Fe, either visiting or making a movie.

Greer Garson bought velvet shirts for herself and her husband, Buddy Fogelson. When we had clothes in the annual Fiesta style show, Exhibicion de Modas, Ms. Garson was often the mistress of ceremonies.

Millicent Rogers' son, Paul Peralta-Ramos, bought a Navajo style outfit and had it shipped to New York. Pop Cholea, a well-known painter, wore Navajo blouses also. We loved our famous customers, many of whom were writers, artists, or actors. They liked to be recognized, but they liked their privacy, too. Most of the time they could have both.

Judy Blume was becoming a successful writer while she lived here. Her children were friends with our grandchildren, and she wore our clothes.

We had Nat Owings and his mother Emily Barnes. Emily would faithfully buy my Navajo skirts and take them home and adjust the waistline to suit her. Nat wore our velveteen shirts.

A walking advertisement was Dickie Pfaelzer, who wore calico ribbon blouses and pleated, three-tiered skirts all the time. Dickie reigned over the Elaine Horwitch Art Gallery and sent us her friends who were visiting.

Mrs. John Adair was an early customer. Her husband has been filming Indians and their silver smithing since 1938.

Another early customer was June Benson, former mayor of Norman, Oklahoma. She grew up at Granite, Oklahoma, and remembered Lone Wolf.

Oklahomans liked my clothes. When a friend, Shirley Campbell, moved to Norman, she was invited to a dinner party. She considered wearing her Navajo style clothes and her silver concho belt. Then she decided it might be too "New Mexico" and chose something more conventional. Was she surprised to find four of the women guests were wearing clothes from the Birdwatcher.

We enjoyed knowing Peggy Pond Church, author of *The House at Otowi Bridge*, a story of the days when Los Alamos was a secret city. Peggy Pond Church spent her girlhood days in Los Alamos. She had a happy, carefree life there. She bought a charming blouse and skirt to wear when she and her husband celebrated their fiftieth wedding anniversary.

Robert Redford and his wife Lola were two of my favorites. He proved to be a very down-to-earth person, kind and considerate. He told me that when a New York tailor offered to copy one of his Bird-watcher velvet shirts, he refused, thinking it would be unfair to me.

Oh, we had a few baddies. Very few when you consider that we were in business for over seventeen years. One of the banks had caused me a loss of more than a hundred dollars. When I talked to them, they passed the buck, looked at me as if they were all wise, and I got nowhere. On the advice of a banker friend, I decided to ask for my money one more time. I said to them, "I'll tell you what I'm going to do. I'm going in there, in that lobby, sit on that couch and when I have my money, I will leave." I went into the lobby and sat down. In about fifteen minutes the clerk presented me with the money.

Another family was well-known for passing worthless checks. When I received one, I began calling and did not get to first base. So I decided to go to the top employer. When the father came in with the cash for his daughter, he said, "She's just a chip off the old block."

Dealing with the public showed us many sides of human nature. When we began to make pleated Navajo skirts, they would say, "Have these come back in style?"

My stock answer was, "They never did go out of style in Santa Fe."

But we also had hundreds of people who were not rude or thoughtless.

"How much do I owe you?"

"How much do your skirts run?"

"If you had it in pink, I'd buy it in a minute."

"How much do you want for this?"

"I bought a dress from you folks last week, and wondered if you had another one like it."

There were those whose motto was, "Love me, love my dog." My friend next door had a large dog she brought to work every day. She told me the dog had bitten one of her customers. I noticed one day that we had few customers, when a lady came in and said that a big white dog was stationed in front of my door. I yelled and scolded it, to no avail. It sat there. I got a yardstick and slapped at it. The dog bit the yardstick. The next step was a big pitcher of water and that worked.

One couple had a dog that went with them on every vacation. They explained that they couldn't go shopping one morning until "Babe" went to sleep so they could slip away. One day they brought Babe and tied her to my wicker rocker and went into the other room to try on clothes. Soon the dog was dragging the rocker into the other room.

Then we had those who used me as baby sitter or mother sitter. A couple from the University of New Mexico came in, looked around, parked mother in a comfortable chair, then slipped away. Mother was in her eighties and as I tried to make conversation, she fell asleep. Much later, the couple returned, showed us their purchases from down the street and said, "Oh, Mother, did you get in a nap or two?"

Another couple left their aged mother on the couch, saying they would be back in a few minutes. After a long, long delay, while the couple shopped on Canyon Road, the mother thought they were not coming back and left. We didn't know where she went!

The climax of this tale was when first Lord & Taylor, then Saks Fifth Avenue, came to town from the big city of New York. These stores were going to remodel a whole floor to be filled with everything from Santa Fe — food, arts and crafts, and of course, clothes. Everything but the mountains. The publicity would put Santa Fe on the fashion map.

In 1981 the rest of the world wanted Santa Fe styles, jewelry, paintings, and weavings, saddles and pottery. The Indian painter, Nieto, went to Paris with a show of his work. His wife wore my velvet Navajo outfits and received as much attention as her husband. Paul Jenkins came from New York and brought me an autographed poster and his wife bought lots of Birdwatcher clothes.

When Lord & Taylor came to buy for their stores, I could not deal with them. I had my hands full with the people of Santa Fe and my regular customers.

Then one day Saks Fifth Avenue appeared in the person of Jessica, their public relations girl. She was Ms. Personality Plus. She had looked over Santa Fe and knew I had the best in velvet Navajo outfits. She managed to persuade me to agree to making a supply in two months. She left saying, 'I'll send the buyer."

A week or so later I was running the shop alone; my help had let me down that day. The phone rang; I answered. I explained that I was alone and couldn't see her that day. I told her, "I thought I was to deal with Jessica."

She said, "Well, maybe I can see you sometime when I'm in your area."

A few days later she appeared with Jessica and placed a $10,000 order.

I found out later that the buyer was within two blocks of me at the Weaving Center when she called. She had said to my weaving friend, Victoria, "That woman! I don't know whether I want to deal with her or not?"

As the deadline for shipment grew near, I started to panic. I got everyone I could to help me. Phoebe Hummel helped with invoices and packing. My husband helped find boxes and pack them. A photographer came. The *New York Times* published that photo on Sunday, November 15, 1981. We got everything sent off in time.

In the late '70's Jim and Barbara decided to leave Houston and move to Santa Fe. They stayed with us while house hunting. One day in October I got word from my friend Lois in Bakersfield, California, that she and her friend Clara Belle were coming to visit. I had known Lois since teenage days and had visited her in Bakersfield, but she had never been able to come to Santa Fe. I told her that we would be happy to have them, but since Jim and Barbara and their three children were living with us, I would put them up at La Posada. I found them a cosy room with a fireplace and kitch-enette. They were a few blocks from the Plaza and not far from the shop. They planned to stay a week.

In the meantime things were more than busy at the shop. I tried to handle it all — extended family, customers, and visitors from

Bakersfield. Jim made pizzas for everyone one evening. We had potluck at their La Posada apartment on night. We made every effort to entertain them.

But somehow they were not impressed with Santa Fe. They didn't like our architecture. They asked, "Do people really live in these houses?" Our sidewalks had cracks in them. "Are people allowed to jaywalk here?"

I took them to the Shed, a favorite local restaurant serving northern New Mexico specialities, for lunch. They talked about a place to eat in Bakersfield that they liked better.

They came up to the shop. When they saw a velveteen Navajo dress on "Sally," our mannequin, Lois asked, "Where would anybody wear a thing like that?"

They didn't like my friends. They talked of going home early. The next day, I had Jim and Barbara run the shop, so I could go with them to Taos. I had just seen a quote in the *Miami Herald:* "When the banks of the Rio Grande and the mountain slopes are covered with shimmering golden aspens, even the most cynical urbanite gets a lump in his throat." Not our visitors from Bakersfield. Some of the more brilliant spots of cottonwoods reminded them of a certain place in California.

Clara Belle had been told by friends that she must be sure to see Taos Pueblo. They remained silent in their observation of Taos and the Pueblo. We came back by way of Espanola. They announced they were leaving early the next morning; they had everything packed. As we drove into the driveway that afternoon, Jim said, "Phone Barbara at the shop and ask her what happened today; just phone her." Lois and Clara Belle sat in the living room while I talked to Barbara.

Her news was that Robert Redford had come in that afternoon wanting one of my velvet shirts. He would be back tomorrow when I would be there.

The trip for the Bakersfield two was saved! They would be leaving early in the morning but could they see a shirt like the one he wanted, so they could tell the folks at home about it. I didn't have one. Could they see some material like it? I looked through my velvet scraps and found a piece and gave it to them.

A week later I got a letter from Lois. She had taken the piece of velvet like Robert Redford's shirt to her church ladies' circle. She passed it around the circle so all the ladies could feel it.

This story came back after some relatives had visited us. They had heard that we were financially secure and successful, and they wanted to see for themselves. They reported to the folks back home that in the living room, the woodwork was heavy mill-sawn, with no framing for the doors. There were iron curtain rods and logs sticking out on the front porch. "Maybe they want it that way," commented one.

"No, I don't think so. They had an old upright piano in the living room, and a leather chair, you know, like you see in Mexico. I just don't know."

"Maybe that is all they can afford."

"Maybe. In the living room was a chest, sort of like a cedar chest, and it had little doodads painted on it. There was a wicked looking Indian with a sword, a beak and feathers, and Indian pots."

When we told our friend Bill Bailey about this report, he said, "Well, I could take care of some of that. I could bring my plane and saw and finish that saw-mill stuff and varnish it."

After seventeen and one-half years at the Birdwatcher, I decided it was time to retire. I was tired and I wanted to make some quilts like the Amish quilts I admired so much. Elbert was also talking retirement. I closed the shop November 1st, 1984.

Our main concern now has to do with world peace. Our children and grandchildren believe as we do that we must fight for peace, that we must do away with the nuclear bomb before it does away with us. We certainly believe that we are not superior to any other races. We are all human beings.

On December the thirtieth in 1985 we celebrated our fiftieth wedding anniversary by going to church and being taken to dinner by our friends, Bill and Gayle Bailey. Our children were scattered everywhere, some of them in foreign countries (Spain, Canada, England, and Colombia), so there was no big celebration. Now we are both retired and although there have been many changes in Santa Fe, we feel that it is a wonderful place to spend the rest of our days.

INDEX